ICEBERG SLIM
The Lost Interviews

By Ian Whitaker

GW00683377

Infinite Dreams
Publishing

Published by
INFINITE DREAMS
info@infinitedreamspublishing.co.uk

Copyright © 2009 Ian Whitaker
First Edition Published 2009

ISBN 978-0-9541355-1-5

Front and back cover photos courtesy of Courtesy PLAYERS Magazine, USA. With special thanks to Misty Beck.

Printed in the UK by CPI Bookmarque, Croydon, CR0 4TD.

Visit the Infinite Dreams web site. Buy unique books retail or wholesale anywhere in the world. News, interviews and more.
www.infinitedreamspublishing.co.uk

If you have information on Iceberg Slim that is not included in this book, please email the author.
ian@infinitedreamspublishing.co.uk

ACKNOWLEDGEMENTS

I would like to express my utmost thanks and appreciation to Misty Beck, Wendy Leigh, Bentley Morriss, Holloway House, Players magazine, Steven Finger of the Los Angeles Free Press, Kalamu ya Salaam, Nichelle Holliday, the Los Angeles Sentinel, Bruce Bolkin of Southland Publishing Inc., Jon Guynn of Pasadena Weekly, Paradise, Mr. Joshua, Patty Galle, Preston Edwards, Faisal Ahmed, Zola Salena-Hawkins, Odie Hawkins, Monroe Anderson, Mark Skillz and Richard Milner. Your contributions have been invaluable and have improved this book for every reader to enjoy.

INTRODUCTION & NOTES

The purpose of this book is to give the reader the opportunity to learn more about the man best known as Iceberg Slim.

I believe that the best way to do this is to put Iceberg, and the people who knew him, directly in front of the reader without the impediment of an interpretive middleman.

The result is a fascinating collection of unabridged interviews with Iceberg Slim himself, which forms the core of the book. They are ordered chronologically and are complemented by several revealing, frank conversations with people who knew him. No attempt has been made to homogenise these unique accounts. Each one is a valuable asset for learning more about him.

Various articles have also been included, giving the inquisitive reader even more context and insight as they are enabled, for the first time, to assess and interpret first-hand information on Iceberg Slim for them self.

Misty Beck, Odie Hawkins and Bentley Morriss were not given the benefit of viewing or discussing the Iceberg Slim interviews that are presented in this book before they spoke to me. In taking this course, I hoped to avoid needlessly influencing their personal accounts. There are two exceptions: the Players article, which Misty already owned a copy of, and the National Observer article, which Bentley already owned.

The quality and size of the images in this book varies according to that of the original photos. The publisher and I took the decision to include certain lower quality images because of their rarity. We hope that they will add to, rather than detract from, the reader's experience.

1918 AUGUST 4th Birth in Cook County Hospital, Chicago, of Robert Lee Maupin (named Robert after his father.)

R is thrown against a wall in disgust by his father, because his mother refuses to abandon him on a church doorstep.

1921 R, aged 3, in Indianapolis Tennessee, is sexually abused by a woman who is babysitting him.

1924 R and his mother are "rescued from actual starvation" by Henry Upshaw who brings them to Rockford, Illinois. Henry owns a cleaning and pressing shop, the only black business in town. R calls him Papa.

1928 R, aged 10, witnesses his mother leave "gentle" Henry for Steve "the snake," whom he learns she has been having an affair with. "This kind wonderful man had only been a tool of convenience."

R, his mother and Steve move to Chicago. R witnesses his mother con his birth father and set him up to be burgled.

Steve threatens to beat and kill R if he doesn't run away from his mother and him. R remains with them.

1929 OCTOBER: The Wall Street stock market crash marks the start of the Great Depression. The number of unemployed climbs to over 13 million during the next few years. Hundreds of thousands become homeless.

1933 R graduates from high school with 98.4 average. He's awarded a scholarship at prestigious all-black college Tuskegee, Alabama.

1935 R is expelled for selling bootleg Whiskey on Tuskegee campus.

R, aged 17, asks 15 year-old June to turn a trick. R

5

Receives $5 from the trick. This is his first act of pimping.

June's would-be second trick reports R to her father. R is charged with "carnal knowledge and abuse." R is sentenced to 12-18 months in Wisconsin Green Bay State Reformatory.

1936 R returns to Milwaukee on parole. His parole officer gives him an IQ test. The result is 175.

R delivers for a drugstore, to satisfy his parole conditions. His mother owns a small, lucrative, beauty salon where he sees pimps getting manicures. "They seemed to be so glamorous and so worldly and so polished and sophisticated, you know? This is what moulded my thinking... I used to just *dream* about being a pimp, having all those sexy women givin' me money!"*

Still on parole, R is charged with Grand Theft of $500. He is sentenced to 2 years in State Prison. "It was there that I got the insatiable desire to pimp. I was a member of a clique that talked of nothing except whores and pimping."

1938 R, aged 19, returns to Milwaukee after 21 months incarceration.

R turns out Phyllis and moves with her to Chicago, leaving his mother in tears. R instructs Phyllis to use the name Mary (his mother's name) if she gets arrested.

1941 DECEMBER: The USA enters the Second World War.

The Great Depression comes to an end.

1944 CHRISTMAS: R visits his mother for the first time since 1938.

1945 The Second World War ends.

1946 R is charged with "white slavery." He is incarcerated in

Leavenworth Penitentiary, Kansas, for 18 months.

1947   R is charged with "armed robbery." He is incarcerated in County House of Correction, Chicago. He avoids a sentence of 5-10 years with a bribe. "We tapped out and got a year apiece in the work house. It was like a prison, only tougher. The joint was filthy. The food was unbelievable." He escapes. "I just couldn't get my skull in shape for another bit. It was too soon after the last."

1948   R moves from Chicago to Lima, Ohio.

R becomes addicted to heroin. "I was a pig for banging speedballs." [Injecting cocaine with heroin.]

1949   One of R's whores attempts to murder him. In self-defense he shoots to kill, but only injures her.

R visits his mother for the first time since 1944.

R moves to Cleveland, Ohio.

There is a post-war sales boom of consumer goods: more people than ever own television sets and cars.

1953   R's mother moves to Los Angeles. She marries a Mr. Beck.

R moves to Seattle.

1957   R, helped by a doctor, kicks his heroin habit. "If I'd kept that habit until 1960, I'd have been a corpse within a week in that steel casket waiting for me."

1958   R spends most of his time reading in bed. "I was ancient as a pimp. The end of my pimping career wasn't far in the future."

1959   R assigns his whores to work in houses ran by madams.

1960   R is recaptured after thirteen years as a wanted escapee. He is incarcerated in the County Jail for 2 months. He is then punished with 10 months of solitary confinement in Cook County House of Correction, Chicago, aka Bridewell Prison. The cell is 8ft deep, 4ft wide, normally used to punish prisoners for up to 5 days.

R's mother is bedridden with heart trouble and diabetes.

1961 APRIL: R is released from the House of Correction.

1962 R has now retired from his life as a pimp.

R changes his surname from Maupin to Maupin Beck, to reflect his mother's current name.

R's mother dies in hospital in Los Angeles.

R and Betty meet. Betty is already pregnant.

1963 JUNE 24th: Betty's first child, Robin Bell Beck, is born. R is Robin's stepfather. Baby Bell was the name of the man "Sweet Jones'" character in *Pimp was based on.* ** Albert "Baby" Bell, was, according to the Chicago Defender, "a stormy petrel, a trafficker in women and petty racketeer… The last of Chicago's bad men."

1965 SEPTEMBER 10th: R and B's first daughter, Camille Mary Beck, is born. She is named Mary after R's mother.

1966 R meets a professor whilst he is selling insecticide. The professor records R recounting his life story on tape, but R changes his mind and writes his own book.

R responds to an ad in the LA Times, by submitting the manuscript of *Pimp* to Holloway House. It's accepted.

1967 JANUARY 17th: R and B's second daughter, Melody, is born. The name Melody appears in *Pimp*, which R was writing when Betty was pregnant with her.

MARCH 6[th:] *Pimp* is published by Holloway House. The copyright registration states the author's name as

Slim Lancaster/Iceberg Slim/Robert Beck. Slim Lancaster is moniker used by R in *Pimp*.

DECEMBER 4th: *Trick Baby* is published by Holloway House. One of the characters in the book is named Camille.

1969 AUGUST 5th: *Mama Black Widow* is published by Holloway House.

1970 R and B's third daughter, Bellissa Misty Beck, is born.

1971 MAY 25th: *The Naked Soul of Iceberg Slim* is published by Holloway House.

1973 JANUARY: *Trick Baby* is released as a film by Universal.

1976 Robert and Betty Beck split.

Reflections album is released on ALA Records. Red Holloway (no connection to the publisher) writes and performs the jazz music.

1977 JANUARY 28th: *Death Wish* is published by Holloway House.

JULY 5th: *Long White Con* is published by Holloway House.

1978 Stated in the introduction and copyright registration (1998) of *Doom Fox* as the date it was written.

1979 JUNE 6th: *Airtight Willie & Me* is published by Holloway House. Several of the stories it includes were previously published in Players International magazine in 1976 and 1977.

1980 R receives fan-mail from Diane Millman.

1982 R and Diane Millman are married.

1983 NOVEMBER 14th: R registers *Iceberg Slim:*

screenplay (267 pages in 2 parts) with the Copyright Office.

1986 OCTOBER: R registers *Shetani's Sister/Rucker: Hollywood Vice*, 297 pages, with the Copyright Office.

1990 R registers *Night Train to Sugar Hill* with the Copyright Office under the name Robert Maupin Beck (for the first time not as Iceberg Slim.) Misty and Camille Beck register the same title in November 2000, stating it to be 142 pages.

1992 APRIL 30th: Robert Maupin Beck dies in Culver City Hospital of liver failure. He is buried at Forest Lawn Memorial Park, Glendale, Los Angeles.

AUGUST: Diane Millman Beck registers *The Last Short Stories of Robert Beck* with the Copyright Office. Date of creation stated as 1990.

1998 OCTOBER: *Doom Fox* is posthumously published in the USA by Grove Press, New York. And in the UK by Cannongate Books.

Pimp is published in Spanish by Anagrama in Spain.

2001 AUGUST: The authenticity of *Doom Fox* is questioned by Camille Beck.

2009 Filming of the Iceberg Slim documentary *Portrait of a Pimp* commences. Directed by Jorge Hinojosa, who is also Ice-T's manager.

---

* From *Answer Me!* Issue 1, by Jim Goad. October 1991. ** Researched by Mark Skillz. All other quotations from *Pimp: the Story of My life.*

AMERICA'S NO.1 PIMP TELLS IT LIKE IT IS!

By Richard B Milner

Rogue Magazine

Issue 18

June 1969

Pimp. A strong word with many meanings. To the moviegoer, a brutish Frenchman with sweaty undershirt and dangling cigarette who slaps women in the face. To the tourist, a Mexican taxicab driver with pencil-line moustache. To the solider, a war-torn child steering to a hovel, whining "Meester, you want my seester?" And to the black man in American ghettos, a charismatic hero whose style and flash were the dream of young shine boys as they polished the hundred-dollar alligator shoes of their idols.

One such ghetto idol was Iceberg Slim. During the thirties and forties in the street jungles of Chicago, Iceberg used women as some men use Kleenex. Before he was old enough to vote he had turned his romantic good looks and his keen intelligence to the profitable task of degrading and brutalizing women.

Iceberg Slim was not the best pimp in Chicago. In fact, as blues singer Jimmy Witherspoon put it, "There are thousands of Iceberg Slims." Yet, today Iceberg is a legend, and most pimps and prostitutes in this country know his name and his deeds. For Iceberg Slim, unlike most pimps who wind up in the jails, the morgues, the back alleys amidst broken wine bottles, and the narcotics hospitals, pulled himself out of the gutter and into a career as a best-selling author.

His book "Pimp: the Story of My Life," published by Holloway House, keeps selling out each printing. Despite scant promotion, at least half a million copies have been sold in the two years since the book was published.

In this remarkable autobiography, Iceberg Slim has given the first honest picture of what pimping is all about, without attempting to romanticize himself or the world in which he moved.

Because the history of pimping in America is so intimately tied to the oppressive conditions of Negro ghetto life, the book also presents nitty-gritty insights into the life of the black man in America. Although the story of his experiences is often repellent, the insightful awareness with which he has told it moves Iceberg Slim into the company of Malcolm X, Claude Brown, Dick Gregory, and other black men who have lived the hard life and then wrote about it with perspective.

Unlike Gregory and Malcolm, however, Iceberg has never used or needed a ghost-writer. For the past several years he has been dedicated to improving his literary skills, although he will never forsake the street language or "soul talk" which gives his books their special authenticity. "The cat on the corner will always be able to understand my books," he says. He writes his books out in longhand, filling thick notebooks with manuscript. His second book, "Trick Baby," also published by Holloway House, is already a success; he is currently working on a third.

On a recent Saturday afternoon I visited Iceberg Slim at his home. Here is a condensation of our three-hour interview:

In your book, you write "A good pimp doesn't get paid for screwing, he gets his payoff for always having the right thing to say to a whore right on lightening tap."

Yes, I also wrote in my book "Pimp" that pimping isn't a sex game; it's a skull game. Do you know what the average tenure of any particular whore with any particular pimp is?

I have no figures.

About a year. Six months, sometimes six weeks. But if he's a good pimp, a year. You know why these whores don't stay long? It's because he sours. When you stop telling a whore something fresh and new and confusing every day – you see, you've got to keep them confused – then she'll leave you, she'll blow. Now, it must not be the kind of confusion that they can detect. But you've always got to keep them in the position where they think that there is a body of knowledge still untapped in your brain. I kept one whore for thirteen years, and that's not the record.

What makes a good pimp?

The fellows in the street – all the good pimps – they say, "You gotta be *born* pimp. The best pimps are born pimps." And it's true. I was never the best of the pimps that I grew up with. The best pimps I know are the pimps that were abandoned by their old ladies – left in garbage cans and in the alleys when they were little, tiny – that never knew any affection or love. These were the fellows that had absolutely no hearts. To be a great pimp, I think you've really got to hate your mother. I always had a "sucker residual." This is why I was able to transfer from pimpin'.

ROGUE asked me to do this interview because I'm doing research for a book on pimps and their world, which pimps call "The Life." So far I've interviewed many practicing pimps, and they all say that once you're in "The Life" you can never really get out of it.

That's what they say, yeah. Hell, I know a pimp sixty years old, and he's still pimping. All the pimps I knew wound up booking horses, in the penitentiary, dying of dope, winos, like that. Except for me, I've never known a pimp to retire gracefully and then go into another profession. Wait a minute, now let me qualify that. I know some half-assed pimps, there are a lot of half-hearted son-of-bitches who have had whores who have been able to open bars and cabarets, but they were never really pimps. You see, the school I came up under, it was a violation of The Book – The *Book* – to accept anything but whore money.

What was The Book?

The Book was the unwritten code of the pimp which was handed down by word of mouth from the older men to the younger dudes. If you ass-kissed one of the older men, took his abuse, he'd say "Alright you little dumb bastard, siddown," and then he'd run down the game to you. They don't have those informal schools anymore. Now it's trial-and-error.

I explained in "Pimp" what the rules of this "skull-book" were, how The Book was "written" by black geniuses in the cities just after slavery times, and how I first learned the tradition from a successful big-city pimp. Anyway, according to that Book you couldn't sell dope, and you couldn't accept any money from boosters [thieves/shoplifters].

How does a pimp utilize that attitude with his "ladies?"

Oh, in many ways. For example, the way he coaches his "get-down" language or dialogue enables me to see immediately what kind of pimp he is. I remember there was a little fellow from Kansas City once who was touted as a great pimp. Oh, his name was ringing in Chicago. So I was up there smoking pot with him and snortin' cocaine. At the "get-down" time he said, "Baby, it's after eight o'clock, don't you think... Don't you *think! Don't* you think!" So I said to myself, "this guy ain't no pimp." A pimp doesn't do that. He says [assuming a nasty, icy voice] "Bitch, you motherfucker, you're five minutes late!" [Resuming normal voice] I mean there are no flaws in the dialogue. There's never much air for the whore. Because if you give her that much air, you've started the process of "blowing," loosing the whore [Laughs] It's gotta be air-tight, Jim, even when you want 'em. It's a prat. You prat, prat.

Do you think that these techniques apply to all women?

You know, I am almost certain that the principles of good pimping apply to all man and woman relationships. Now let's cancel out, of course, the physical and overt thing that the pimp used to do. But the cruelty must be there in a successful relationship between a man and a woman, even if it's only subtle psychological cruelty. You must appeal to that degree of masochism within even a square broad. Of course, the degree depends on their sensitivity and culture and background. But they all like a *little* cruelty.

Would you say that there is a real war between the sexes, then?

Oh, constantly. If the man doesn't keep the upper hand then the woman will take over. And then she doesn't want him any more; she wants to try another challenge. Once she's sure, once she's ever sure of you...

With all your experiences with all kinds of women, what advice would you give to the American male on how to pursue and get and keep a woman?

I would advise not to pursue but to stalk, first of all. Or, should I say not to chase, but to stalk. And when you cop, don't clutch. Give her her head, let her come and go as she pleases, and you'll keep 'em a long time.

And don't ever show jealousy, because when you start showing jealousy you're showing insecurity. And when you show insecurity, you're going to blow.

What do you think jealousy is?

It's insecurity. It's not love, that's a cinch, because love has nothing to do with jealousy. And an intelligent woman knows it right away. It has no part, it has no relationship to love at all. It's a selfish motivation.

Of course, most American men get completely incensed at the thought of their woman making it with somebody else, and I think many men must wonder how a pimp can let his women make it with all those men and not be jealous.

He has no choice, really. [Laughs] He has no choice. He's got to have money. Even if he should be stupid enough to get weak for his whore, he certainly can't show it. Otherwise he's going to loose her. Or else she'll say [imitates woman] "Well, I'm gonna square up [stop whoring and seek marriage] if you love me that much, you simple motherfucker, you." So the only thing he can do is suffer in silence and take that money. That's all he can do – so he's in a hell of a bind. [Laughs]

No, you can't afford to be jealous. That's the quickest way to blow a woman, whether she's a whore or square. Jealousy. Because then you become paranoid – it's a thing that builds up. You plant a little seed there, let it grow, and it will kill you.

Most of the pimps I have interviewed frankly admit that they are in the game for the money. Was that your motivation?

No, we did it for the thrill. Because there is the most transcendental ecstasy in the vilification of a woman - that's where the thrill was. The money! I didn't care about the money – it was in the absolute vilification, in the degradation. I had this intense hatred, don't you see? This need! This was the motive force that made me a pimp – to *vilify!* I *lost* all the money, threw it away, and shot it in my arm. I know these fellows today are pimpin' for the money, but we didn't pimp for the money. We pimped because we *loved* to pimp.

By the way, was "Iceberg Slim" really your nickname on the streets?

No, I made up the name "Iceberg Slim" as a synthesis of the whole thing – the coldness, the icy attitude and outlook and practice. I use it as my pen-name now.

Do you have any regrets about the life you lived – or did you dig it all?

No, I don't have any regrets. Except I wish I hadn't gotten caught so often. [Laughter] I wish I could have spent more time in the street, wish I hadn't had to spend all that time in "durance vile." You know, the last time I was in the penitentiary they tried their best to kill me, locked me up in a steel casket to die, just like I told in my book. That finished pimping for me for good.

But pimping was an idiot's paradise anyway, and I'm ecstatic that I left it and the steel casket behind. Now don't get me wrong; I still feel a little twinge of nostalgia when I pass and see some lissome lass hustling up and down Western and I remember the old days. When I see her making mistakes I want to tell her. Or when I see some youngster in his El Dorado taking his money on the street, or taking it after each trick instead of letting it accumulate. Little things like that, then I want to involve myself, you know.

And, let's face it, any old pimp wants to advise – just like anything else – he wants to stick his nose in and talk with the youngsters. But as far as pimpin', man, I don't want to pimp. I want to be a good writer. I'm coming out of there. And I'm agonizing now with my writing. I'm seeking to do in sentences what it took me paragraphs to do before, and to do in one word what it took me sentences to do in these books.

Writing books is better than pimping. In fact, it's better than being a doctor or a lawyer. I don't have to go to court, I don't have to go to the hospital to perform an operation. I have no equipment, man. Look, I don't even need paper; I'll write on the walls. All of my equipment [tapping his head] is in my noggin. And another thing: writing has been a wonderful boon for me, psychologically. The vacuum of ego that existed when I could no longer pimp has been filled most adequately.

Do you think all pimps are egomaniacs?

Oh, they got to be, they got to be. See? And that's why when a pimp is no longer pimping he's in such bad psychological straits, he's in trouble.

What did pimps do while their broads were out? They never would solicit...

Oh no, God no. No, that's no good for that thing I was telling you about – inside you. You can't steer a whore to a trick, can't do that. As I said before, pimping is a *feeling*. If I was going to screw around and ass off and have sissies and clown and bullshit I wouldn't have wanted to be a pimp. Pimps had class man.

Did the pimps spend a lot of time with other pimps – in bars, snorting cocaine, hanging around?

A lot of them did that, but I spent a lot of time alone, reading. Strangely enough I used to go to the library and I used to go to the bookstores and buy psychiatric books, all the works of Freud, and books on philosophy. And I never let the other pimps know that I had a yen for that kind of thing because they would have said "Oh, he's a square. Man, what the..."

Why does a whore stick with a pimp when he treats her badly and takes all her money?

A whore really goes for a pimp, gives him her money and endures what he puts on her because of the sense of importance that she gets from his notoriety and saying "So-

17

and-so is my man." She is so bereft and so insecure, and needs to shine. She'll settle for even *this* kind of fake acclaim.

Isn't that true to some extent of all women? Any square housewife – often the reason they will do things for their man is because of the reflected glory of the association, to be able to say, "He's my man?"

Yes, that's true, but they won't take that kind of punishment for it; that's the difference. And there's another reason, too, for whores getting hooked: there's an ego-satisfaction. Every time a trick [customer] pays a whore – and I've watched 'em, I've watched 'em – it's ego-satisfying to them. Particularly to just an ordinary broad who has been able through the magic of false eyelashes, a wig, lots of makeup and some flashy clothes to transform herself, so that in the course of one night twenty different men, including big-shots with nice business suits on, will actually pursue her and give her money. That phoney ego build-up is a kind of substitute for love – that's what it really is – because she ain't gonna get none from the pimp.

I don't care how much a pimp protests "I love you, baby," a whore knows, instinctively a whore knows. See. How can you possibly...? A whore knows that you can't. And how can a whore love a pimp – when he's constantly taking and not giving up anything?

The pimps I have interviewed say that they're the only "real men" in America because they can control women and make fools out of the white men. Some even consider themselves more clever than the Black Panthers and other militants because instead of confronting the white man, they take his money and his women.

Pimps are always talking about their manhood, but, let's face it, a pimp doesn't have any manhood. He doesn't have any. What's manly about being supported by a woman and giving nothing in return? Anybody who pimps, in my estimation, is involving himself in the most useless and unprofitable profession, one that can land him in the penitentiary, or that can put him in a grave prematurely.

So he's copping the white man's woman and "turning her out." So what? I mean, how much courage and cunning does it take? He's not hurting the white man that's doing him the wrong in this country by taking the social dregs and "turning them out!" [Making them into his whores.]

And, sure, he's taking the white man's money, but he's not taking it in quantities and from the people who are really hurting him – that clique, that clique at the top who control the important money and the government in this country. He's not hurting them. He's hurting jokers that are in the same boat, practically, that he's in. You dig it?

Now, getting to the Panthers and other militants. It's a crying shame that the black militant groups of today have nothing but contempt for older black men. You can make an effort to be in their company and perhaps give them counsel, but they will turn away from the wisdom that you perhaps possess. Right off the top of my head I think the most perfect strategy that the black militants could have employed would have been to stay underground.

Since the Panthers have so much moxie, since they're not afraid to die, since they're capable of projecting great terror, why didn't they go underground and for a completely secret organization, with a spy network and all? They could take over this whole country and no one would stop them. If the white man heard that an elaborate black espionage organization existed he would think, "No nigger is that smart" and go back to sleep. But these youngsters have no time to listen to older black men.

How did you get into pimping anyway?

I had a chance in life not to get hooked with pimping or anything else, if I just hadn't got that time when I was eighteen. If they had given me probation then, I might not have bit, man. But in the "joint" [prison] I heard all that game [pimp's shoptalk] man. That's what really did it – heard too much game, man. And then the Depression.

And then, you see, I saw those pimps in these long Packards – at that time the Packard was the flash car – and these long yellow triple-A shoes. God, those fellows! And rings, like hunks of rainbow on their fingers. I used to see them. *God.* I wanted to be a pimp.

I hear they used to have big national "conventions," I haven't seen any of that.

19

Oh, yeah, they used to, really… when they had funerals. I remember a funeral once in Detroit, when Rabbit died in Detroit. They threw reefer and cocaine into his grave. One broad, one of his whores was drunk at the gravesite. She said, "Oh, Daddy, your bitch ain't gonna let you go. Your bitch ain't gonna let you go by yourself! Bury me with Daddy!" And that bitch threw herself in the grave, you know?

What were the best towns for pimps?

Well, San Francisco was pretty good for me. Detroit, Cleveland, Rochester, New York – I think those are the best towns in the country. Of course, the town where I had to shoot that broad – oh it was awful! She's rich now, broad got rich in the very house that I shot her. I had to shoot her. She had a history of murder. [His children interrupt to say that they are going to the store and want to know if he wants anything. He replies with elaborate courtesy, "No, thank you."]

Now isn't that… see, what are you going to do? Now, what the hell! What if you told me that in the steel casket? See what I'm saying. Look, I have absolutely skunked every pimpin' bastard that ever did it. What other bastard has been able to get all the thrills of pimpin' and then get all the thrills and excitement of a family – all within one lifetime!

It's like two lifetimes, really!

Even the excitement of dope. [Rolls up sleeve to show needle scars on his arm] Who? Is there one in life? Is there? …follow me? …pimpin'! Family! All within one lifetime! See my kids? You see me, I'm Papa! [Laughs with delight] What the hell! I'm right here *with* it!

I clearly remember during the interview that when he said Iceberg Slim was not his name in the streets, he told me that the name he did use was Cavanaugh.
Richard Millner

From conversations with Ian Whitaker 2009.
20

CHICAGO LOCALE FOR "ICEBERG SLIM" MOVIE

Chicago Defender

8th September 1971

Chicago recently was the scene of the filming of a 20 minute documentary entitled "Iceberg Slim: Up From Under." According to NET Black Journal producer-director William Gaddis, the film "deals with the negative glamour of the hustler and his life using Robert Beck (Iceberg Slim), author, essayist and ex-pimp as the main "character."

The all-black production features dramatization of a pimp's life and exclusive interview with Iceberg Slim. The film is aimed at highlighting the degradation of a hustler's life in an effort to discourage young blacks from seeking "the pimp's way."

Director Gaddis and author Beck expressed admiration for the strength that is required for a black man to exist as a hustler, but hope that the film will show blacks that hustling is not in the best interest of blacks building a nation. The film will be aired on Black Journal in the fall.

The two Iceberg Slims... Actor Alade Alabukon, who portrays Iceberg Slim, and Robert Beck, the real Iceberg Slim, watch filming of the all-black production. Chicago was selected for the site of filming because much of Iceberg Slim's hustling career was spent here.

Detained at tavern front... Beck makes his point to Angela Fontanez, assistant to producer Bill Gaddis in front of Gerri's Palm Tavern on 47th street. The Palm Tavern served as one of Iceberg's hangouts during his hustling life.

Actors for dramatic parts of the film were supplied by Chicago's Kuumba workshop.

Rapping to the students... Displaying the form that rated him as one of the nation's top pimps, Iceberg runs down the degradation he experienced as a pimp to Malcolm X College students.

"Use your head..." In a special "rap" at Malcolm X College, Iceberg Slim urges the black student body to re-examine their adoration for hustlers, pimps and junkies by looking more closely at the sickness that was his life.

Author of five books... The author of four books and a book of essays, Beck cautions black people to seriously begin the process of nation-building and to cast away the shackles of slavery that hustling and pimping bring.

1971. Iceberg Slim and actor Alade Alabukon in Chicago during the filming of the "Iceberg Slim: Up From Under" documentary.

NO MORE BAUBLES

Onetime Procurer Iceberg Slim
Turns to Prose – and Still Sells

By Monroe Anderson

The National Observer

4th December 1971

For a quarter of a century, Iceberg Slim got his kicks from punishing prostitutes. Conservatively, he guesses he managed more than 400 women during that time. He also had new Cadillacs every year, four stints in Federal and state prisons, a heartbroken mother, an experience in which he shot and nearly killed one of his whores, and a heroin habit.

Iceberg Slim was a top-echelon pimp on Chicago's South Side. Now he's a top-selling writer.

"This is the story of my life." Says Robert Beck, who writes under the name Iceberg Slim. "I've always been able to turn apparent disaster into an advantage."

The disaster, he says, was his once-misdirected talents. But today, more than 2,000,000 copies of his four books are in print, with two of them, *Trick Baby* and *Pimp: the Story of My Life*, possibly becoming movies soon. He also has a one-man crusade going to expose what he calls the "negative glamour" of pimping and the "white racist power structure" that he says perpetuates it.

How He Began

Beck's transition began 10 years ago. At age 43, a time when most men are at the peak of their careers, Beck was getting too old for pimping. While completing 11 months due on his fourth jail sentence, interrupted a few years earlier by his escape, Beck was faced with the decision of returning to The Life or seeking a new and possibly legitimate employment.

"I realised I had been stupid," he says, although prison psychiatrists told him he had an IQ of 175. "I was elderly and tired. I had the revelation that pimping, after all, was not the

25

most magnificent profession. I had a feeling that I had wasted myself."

So he retired and left Chicago for Los Angeles, where he spent the last six months of his ailing mother's life at her oxygen-tent-covered bedside. He was trying to right the wrongs he had done her, he says, which were responsible for her failing health – and to nurture a love that prison psychiatrists explained had previously been hate. Shortly after his mother's death in 1962, Beck was married and became a $75-a-week insecticide salesman. "After all," he says, "I had been a natural salesman all my life."

Racing the Professor

While making a sales pitch to a college professor four years later, Beck revealed he was a former pimp. Intrigued, the professor proposed that they collaborate on Beck's biography. Beck agreed, but after the interview taping was over, he discovered he would get a minimal percentage of the book's royalties.

"The professor had all the recorded material. I wanted to beat him to the wire." Beck says. "I wanted to deprive him of doing the book without me."

He did. Using the former professor's potential book as a challenge, Beck finished his first book, *Pimp*, in three months. Once again he turned apparent disaster to his advantage. "All I had to do, of course, was just remember," he admits. "There wasn't any real creativity."

But there were perception and retrospect, for in the book, Beck bares his mind and the pimp psychology to the reader while writing in the argot of the ghetto with descriptions to match. And while young blacks aspiring to become pimps call Beck's book "The Bible," its definitive anti-pimping tone is exemplified in this passage:

"The whores went into fits of giggles at Rachel's shaky witticism. A pimp is happy when his whores giggle. He knows they are still asleep."

Beck sees similarities between writing and pimping. "The same technique that I used to make logical to a whore the necessity of being my woman, I use in my writing to be convincing," he explains. "All the motivations in fiction are the same as those in The Life." Writer and pimp, he says, share self-starting drive, tenacity, insight, knowledge of human character, logic and the will to endure a lonely existence.

After *Pimp*, Beck's next book dealing with the life of pimps and prostitutes was his third, *Mama Black Widow*. But that is where the similarity ends. In *Widow* Beck puts his old knowledge into a different head: the pimp this time is a female homosexual. "I knew if I were really to become a writer – and I'm still learning – I had to develop some sort of versatility," he says.

Sponging Information

That's why his second book, *Trick Baby*, is a novel about a mulatto con man. Beck spent some time in jail with the con man and was taught all the secrets of the game. "I've made myself a sponge throughout my life," he says "I learned all the intricacies of burglary and the con game. Most of my life was spent with people and in situations where the Mafia was around."

Beck's knowledge of the Mafia and how drugs enter and are sold in the United States is the source of his next novel, which he is now writing. It deals with a group of super black activists, evolved from the Black Panthers, who set out to destroy the Mafia's business in the black community, beginning with Chicago's South Side.

The book is obviously political. But that is Beck's current direction, away from pimps, prostitutes and sheer entertainment. His fourth book, *The Naked Soul of Iceberg Slim*, is a collection of essays on his new life and the political climate in America as he sees it. "I wrote *Naked Soul* as a position paper," he says. "Prior to that there had been no real empathy with the characters in my writing. But these are times when you must choose sides if you're going to be a black writer."

Recently, in a lecture at Malcolm X College in Chicago that was filmed for *Black Journal* television show, he said "The pimp is an ill man and I think he should be treated as an ill man – as a victim of this racist white society that makes street poisoning possible."

Beck writes up to 18 hours a day, often long past the time when his wife Catherine and four children are in bed. "My style is different," he says, "but it turns out I reach the masses of black people – and white people too. If my style were more brilliant and more convoluted, they wouldn't dig me. If I were really educated, I'd be in trouble. Even the flaws in my writing are an advantage: the uninhibited approach. I tell the truth. When I do something stupid I report it."

Summing up, he says, "Writing is the only thrill for me now. I was split from the black movement. I considered baubles – I'm talking about the cars and crap – more important than my people. I want to alleviate the great guilt I feel for the waste of my life."

I interviewed Iceberg while taking notes. The phone was cradled to my neck à la All the President's Men *style. And, the notes I took are long gone. Besides the interview you see, he spent a lot of time telling me about the psychologies of both pimps and hookers. I found it absolutely fascinating, but it was nothing I could put in a family newspaper.*
Monroe Anderson

From correspondence with Ian Whitaker 2009.

Early 1940s. Iceberg Slim in his 20s, possibly next to Party Time.

Courtesy of Misty Beck.

THE INSIDE STORY OF BLACK PIMPS

By Bob Moore

Sepia Magazine

February 1972

Suddenly the black pimp has made it big – in movies, plays and books. The legends and stereotypes, the long-time racist chatter and the hushed malicious hearsay about fantastic sexual acrobatics have emerged into the open – and the black pimp is now glorified on stage and screen and literature... and even accepted as some kind of folk hero by the mindless and unknowing.

The austere New York Times reports in a sobering chronicle on the lives of big city prostitutes that 95 per cent of pimps in New York are black... and its portrait of the black pimp is not entirely unkindly.

To at least one pimp, now retired and an accomplished author with four published books to his credit, the new respectability of the pimp is both humorous and tragic. His name is Iceberg Slim, or at least it was then when he worked the streets, but he was born Robert Beck. To him the humour is in the new aura of seeming esteem for pimps; the tragedy is that in his eyes pimping is racism in the raw and both pimps and prostitutes are "victims of the white racist society."

But a Pulitzer Prize-winning play, Charles Gordone's "No Place To Be Somebody," and Melvin Van Peebles' controversial movie "Sweet Sweetback's Badasssss Song" and a new Broadway Production, "Ain't Supposed To Die A Natural Death," all have spotlighted the black pimp and idolized him in a sense, endowing him with a distinction of sorts.

Whatever else is said about Iceberg Slim's reports on the black pimp, however, he cannot be accused of exalting the black pimp, even though in true pimp style, he was able to cash in richly on his pimping by writing on his career in the streets. Iceberg Slim, as portrayed by Iceberg Slim, is quite a despicable character from the opening words of his best seller – "Dawn was breaking as the big hog scooted through the streets. My five whores were chattering like drunk magpies. I smelled the stink that only a street whore has after a long, busy night." And so it goes for 317 pages in his paperback, "Pimp," that has sold almost one million copies since it was published five years ago. The book is perhaps honest, but also extremely revolting, obscene, repetitive and inevitably boring as most X movies. There is nothing sensual about the sex, nothing particularly distinguished about the writing.

But "Pimp" is a big book in the gutter library of a West Coast publisher and its one unquestioned virtue is that it has enabled Iceberg Slim to go straight. Quite immodestly, Iceberg boasts today: "Except for me, I've never known a pimp to retire gracefully and then go into another profession. All the pimps I knew wound up booking horses, in the penitentiary, dying of dope, winos, like that."

As to what made him decide to "square up" and change his lifestyle, the ex-pimp explains "I was apprehended for escaping from prison when I was 40, which is elderly for a pimp. I had the chance to really examine, while confined, the whole rotten tapestry of my life. And, of course, there was my mother's terminal illness in California. And, there was my overwhelming guilt. I had neglected her, you see, and I was conscious of it. I was at the age where I was no longer blinded by the excitement of pimping. You see, pimping is exciting only when you're learning and when you're young. After you're older, say 35 or 40, it's no longer a thrill. The Eldorados, the diamonds, the clothes, it's only equipment."

Anyone who reads Iceberg Slim's first book recognizes him during his pimping days as a cold-blooded so-and-so. Since his release from prison in 1960, he has lived in Los Angeles and has become a very warm and likable individual. He would hardly seem the same person who, several years earlier, could whip a young prostitute with a wire coat hanger, even though she was ill, for not "humping" and bringing in enough money. Now an author, Iceberg Slim is a respectable family man with a wife, an 8-year-old son and three daughters, ages 7, 4 and 1.

Asked how he could marry after having been so cold-blooded and hard-hearted toward the 400 women he managed, he replies: "I got married because I found a woman who obviously has a lot of common sense and who understands the kinds of changes that I was going through, and who is highly intelligent and extremely lovable, and who just seems to understand - has a sixth sense about what I had gone through.

And, then there was a vacuum there. Mama had died and I needed that kind of care – that kind of understanding. I also had a selfish reason for getting married. I knew that as poisoned as I had been, I had to do something positive – take a positive step out and away from. I had to do some dramatic personal act which would afford some sort of insulation between my still sick brain and the streets and pimping. And I knew that marriage with that kind of responsibility – the prospect of children – would help me.

I had a great fear of becoming one of the older pimps. I've seen so many older pimps well past their prime. How pathetically they attempt to pimp. But, above all, I have deep feelings of love, affection and tenderness for this woman."

Though he has completely abandoned "the life," as pimps refer to pimping, Iceberg Slim still maintains some of the mannerisms of the pimp. At 52, he is quite handsome, dashing, and very glib. According to one young Los Angeles woman, "He is absolutely one of the most fascinating men I've ever met." He wears expensive and flashy clothes and always carries a sponge powder puff with which he makes sure his face is never shiny. He stands 6'2½ tall and weighs a lean 170 pounds. He is extremely dramatic as he makes swift hand and body gestures while he talks.

In all of his books, Iceberg attempts to discourage young men from the pimp life by describing the frustration, the horrors and the futility of it. Yet, because of the glamour and the color of his life, many would-be pimps idolize him. Having made a complete change from the life he lived during the 30's and 40's in the streets of Chicago, Iceberg Slim takes advantage of every opportunity to describe the utter waste of the pimp life.

Speaking of its insecurity, he says: "You become more insecure the older you get. Just like a whore becomes insecure. That's the worst thing, the most traumatic thing about pimping and whoring.

Because a pimp, when he gets old, he doesn't have any charm. He gets hard. There's no more smile, no joke, no play, no humor for a whore. Dig? But a young stud, he's making mistakes. That's why he has charm. But an older pimp gets his game so tight that he won't smile unless there's a lot of money. A broad gives him a big sting, he'll hold his cheek down for a kiss. If the money ain't right, he'll pull away."

In his books, Iceberg Slim is not above philosophizing in sweeping words like those at the beginning of his latest work: "I want to say at the outset that I have become ill, insane, as an inmate of the torture chamber behind America's fake façade of justice and democracy. But I am not as ill as I was and I am getting better all the time."

In speaking of his mental illness, Iceberg says: "I think anybody is insane who has reached the state of mind where he has difficulty relating to people as individuals. Of course, I'm almost well now. I can relate to people. I no longer have the attitude, for instance, when I meet a white person – I no longer say to myself, 'This bastard! How long will it take this SOB to show his ass?' There are levels of degrees of suspicion. Mine was extreme. Mine was so extreme, when I'd go to white firms to apply for positions as salesman, my hostility was so obvious that they could sense it. I never smiled, I couldn't strike an affable attitude and posture. I was like a steel spring, you see; and naturally, you radiate this kind of thing.

Another part of my insanity is that I have terrible nightmares which have now receded somewhat. I used to have hallucinations during the first year after I got out. I used to dream that there would be puffy, green streaked bladders. And they would be rushing in chaos. And, I had a subjective attachment to them, because I was fearful that they would collide. They were all tied to my own existence."

As punishment for a prison escape, which he outlines in his first book "Pimp," when Iceberg was re-captured in 1960, he claims he was locked in a steel box, which was no larger than two arms length in any direction, for ten months. Prison officials at Chicago's House of Correction would be quick to deny the existence of any steel box for prisoners, let alone the condemnation of a man to it for ten months. But it makes good reading in his book, when Iceberg Slim says that the pimp died in that steel box, and a writer was born.

Having read books on psychology and psychiatry during a stretch at Leavenworth Penitentiary, Iceberg has been able to cope with his own "insanity." He explains: "I had done all that reading in Leavenworth – psychiatric – terribly complicated. After all, I don't have formal education. I just did graduate from high school. But, I always daydreamed in school."

The new writer reluctantly admits he has an I.Q. of 175. "I only wish," he admits, "I had understood my potential when

I was younger and channelled my energies into more constructive areas. I was actually much quicker in multiple areas when I was younger, because my mind was unfettered with criminal intent. You see, when a young individual has not become street poisoned – in other words, he has not devoted all his intellectual energies to becoming a pimp, for instance, or to becoming a stick-up man, then he can use his mind constructively. But, when a young mind has become street poisoned, the individual can think of nothing else but his own particular chosen criminal pursuit."

Iceberg Slim is a pseudonym or pen name Robert Beck adopted which he feels fits his cold-blooded nature. "The word iceberg," he explains, "presents a picture of what the real pimp epitomizes." He explains that in order to be a good pimp, one has to be cold-blooded. "The best pimps are born pimps," he contends. "I was never the best pimp of the pimps that I grew up with. The best pimps I know are the pimps that were abandoned by their old ladies – left in garbage cans and in alleys when they were tiny – that never knew any affection or love. These were the fellows that had absolutely no hearts. To be a great pimp, I think you've really got to hate your mother. I always had a sucker residual. This is why I was able to transfer from pimping."

Iceberg displays no modesty when discussing his writing talent: "When I wrote 'Pimp,' all my writing was intuitive. Somehow, it just seemed that the structure was intuitively right. You know, all the things that a writer should have done for his audience, I just did intuitively.

What I did with my first book, I simply made a transfer. I knew that in presenting ideas to whores, or to anybody else, that one had to create a certain kind of situation. In other words, it had to be entertaining. Like when you're talking to a whore, you have to fascinate her. I also knew that you had to be logical. I also knew that it had to be tied up in a neat package – that is, no loose ends. And, you had to answer, just as you do the whore, all of the questions before they are asked. And, you can't be heavy handed with it. You have to do it in a casual way. But I didn't know this was what they call painless exposition that the writing craft speaks about. For every principle that I used in 'Pimp,' there's a literary name."

After having lived a life of excitement, fear, done prison terms, torture, frustration and grief, Iceberg Slim has finally found happiness. His family and his writing take up all of his time. He is extremely proud of and grateful for his transformation. "What other pimp," he asks, "has been able to get all the thrills and excitement of a family – all within one lifetime?"

Negotiations are currently under way to make movies from two of Iceberg Slim's books, "Pimp" and "Mama Black Widow."

Quotes from Iceberg Slim

"I am free of the street poison where I exploited black queens."

"If you exploit your own kind you're, in effect counter-revolutionary."

"By all odds I should have ended a broken shell or died in a prison."

"I feel pride in survival and miracle that I'm not a marooned wreck."

ICEBERG SLIM IS WARMING UP TO LIFE

Reformed Procurer Tells the Story of Tension, Toil and Degradation

By Joe Ellis

Chicago Defender

16th December 1972

"Pimping is an illness. And you can't be a successful pimp unless you're really ill," said Iceberg Slim in an interview at the Daily Defender's offices.

Iceberg Slim is a reformed pimp and doing well. For a quarter of a century he was the cool dude with the ice water running through his veins (which is how he got his name), who lived a life of successful degradation as a pimp on Chicago's Southside, issuing orders to his hundreds of women in his small but bustling-with-action world.

He became affluent, drove expensive cars, and was on to heroin and cocaine. He also was jailed four times in various federal and state prisons, and his mother is said to have died of a broken heart.

Iceberg Slim began a process of self-reformation about 11 years ago, the last time he was released from prison. He quit the existence he once led, describing it as a waste and himself as a "stupid sucker," although prison psychiatrists had told him he had an IQ of 175.

"I'm trying now to reach not only young people but that highly susceptible group of guys who may think that a respectable kind of life is somehow not wonderful. I try to get over the hard fact that there is nothing but pressure, tension, and unpleasant things connected with doping, boosting and having a lot of broads. Really there's nothing to it," he said.

"Some guys are looking for something that's totally destructive. And to envy a pimp or dope pusher or someone with a big front – it's foolish. I've been there and I know. It's not worth the trip. Soon a person who is in it realizes that he's just a sucker for even making the trip or for even wanting to be slick."

"Pimping is destructive because a black pimp's pawns are young black women for the most part, who are potentially

37

the mothers and the very root of the black family structure. We know that the black family structure is on the onslaught from destructive racism in America. But in support of pimping and black pimps, in my opinion they are the only black men in America that because of their way of life, they still are the only ones that are free of that oppression that most black men are under," Iceberg said.

"He is the only black figure who defies all of the restrictions placed on black people. He exploits white women, he thumbs his nose at the powers that be, and he's made himself immune by taking the risk of imprisonment and the rest of it. He enjoys maximum freedom within the society. The average black man has to deal with his inhibitions and restrictions of morality, and conventional ways of society. I have just recently, in the latter part of my life, been able to develop the inhibitions of the average man. They are oppressed heroes, in a limited context, who stand with their (psychological) balls intact," he asserted.

Iceberg, aged 43 when he was released from prison and tore himself loose from his pimp's guise, journeyed to Los Angeles, where he still lives, and spent the last six months of his mother's life at her bedside, seeking atonement.

Iceberg Slim and Robert Beck are one and the same person, but each has a life of his own. At his mother's bedside, he once again assumed the identity of Robert Beck. Beck is a married man with four children and is an author. His novels command a reading public of 2,000,000 people, establishing him in literary circles as the largest selling black author in America. He has written four novels: "Pimp: the Story of My Life." "Mama Black Widow," "Trick Baby" and "The Naked Soul of Iceberg Slim."

As Iceberg Slim, he covers the colleges of the country lecturing to students. "I want to alleviate the great guilt I feel for the waste of my life." He says.

After relocating in Los Angeles, Beck worked as an insecticide salesman. During the course of calling on customers, he met a college professor who heard of the salesman's past and suggested they collaborate on a book.

"The professor has all the recorded material on tape when I realized that I was only going to receive a minimal percentage of the book's royalties," Beck says, "I wanted to do the book without him – and I did."

"I have turned disaster into advantage, writing about what I knew of my former era and the people involved in it," Iceberg says with pride. "I see similarities between writing and conning people."

Of his four novels, the first to reach the screen is "Trick Baby," a drama of a pair of black con men and the suckers they frame, opening December 20th at the Loop Theater.

Beck is in Chicago to make a personal appearance at the movie's premiere, which stars Kiel Martin and Mel Stewart, and co-starring Dallas Edward Hayes, Beverly Ballad and Vernee Watson. A Marshal Backler-James Levitt production, the movie was filmed mainly on the streets of Philadelphia's black ghetto under the direction of Larry Yust. The picture was released by Universal.

"This film has the artistic values that so many black critics of so-called contemporary black films have decried a lack of," Beck asserted. "I think this flick was put together so well that these characters are human beings rather than just super-niggers on the screen moving from one violent scene to another."

"Mel Stewart, who plays Blue Howard in the film, is out of sight. He almost hypnotizes the audiences with his acting. He really becomes Blue Howard on the screen," Slim said. "What makes this flick so unique and compelling to the audiences is the fact that it shows the black con men in action, and it reduces all of the convoluted dynamics existing between a relationship of a victim and the conman. Any member of the audience can readily understand and appreciate some of the psychological happenings going on both inside the victim and the con men. It has all of the excitement and suspense of that spider-fly encounter, the trapping and catching of the victim," Beck asserted with pride.

Beck is now in the process of writing a screenplay for "Pimp," to be released next year and probably filmed in Chicago.

Circa 1953. Iceberg Slim perhaps aged 35.

Courtesy of Misty Beck.

BLACK PLAYERS: THE SECRET WORLD
OF BLACK PIMPS

By Christina and Richard Milner

1972

Deference to males, subservient females

A pimp should be a god to his ladies, according to The Book. "When we pimped," said Iceberg Slim, "there really was a difference: from the HEART, from the absolute heart! Every morning for thirty years I'm looking into the mirror. I never made a mistake, never got Georgiaed [taken advantage of sexually without receiving money]. I'm looking in the mirror. "No mistakes! Clear day! Oh, you slick pimp motherfucker." Used to talk to myself, like a psychotic. You're a psychotic when you're a good pimp. You gotta be. And as I said, it projects, man. Who can stand, I mean what lowly little whore can resist GOD? For Chrissake!"

An old style pimp in the Chicago ghetto during the 1930s, Iceberg lived a hard-and-fast life which was almost cut short by seven years in the penitentiary. Now middle-aged and still good looking, he lives a quiet, sequestered life in Los Angeles with his wife and young children. He is a sensitive and perceptive observer of the world from which he came, and his autobiography, *Pimp: the Story of My Life* is a paperback best-seller which is widely read by people in The Life. Iceberg is delighted that the joys of square family life are now his, with his pimping career long behind him and a continuing career as a writer ahead. His comments often serve as a baseline against which we may view the remarks of younger informants still in The Life. Today, as in Iceberg's day, although The Book has undergone some change and relaxation of the rules, it is still said that a pimp is supposed to be a god to his woman:

JAMES: Each one thinks how their man is God, do you understand? How beautiful that is? I told you about this cat who had... this is what starts leaning my mind in that direction. I started seeing things anew. He went horseback riding with two of his ladies and the horse reared up at him. The horse said [makes a horse sound] and they were explaining this whole scene to me, you know, at the Fairfield restaurant. They say, "Can you imagine, a horse ran after my man, wasn't that something? He might have killed that horse." Now here they are thinking their man is so great he can just take a blow in his hand and kill a horse and knock him down and "How dare you harass me, horse, I'm a MAN!" That's how much they respect and love and dug him as a man at that time. The same girl one year and a half later said to me just two weeks ago, "I hate his mouth, he's ugly, he's horrible, how could I have liked him at all?" But the time she loved him, baby, she would even put a horse against her man. A powerful, muscular, symmetrically beautiful constructed horse with all the power in the world against a single, nobody, pip-squeak man who ain't nothing, but it was her god, her man. And that's what they got over some women... isn't that true? That's the pimp game. It's a good foundation. Now what you do with the foundation is where you are as people. People get hung up and they start to evolve into animals and gangsters and so-called slick people and all that, and destroying each other. But the pimp game has a foundation that everybody should learn about.

Godlike male control is not exclusively a front for others to see. It is a reality in daily life, as the following report by a female informant suggests.

TANYA: When my brother [who is a pimp] wakes up in the morning he can't stand to see her look ugly. In the first place they don't sleep together, they got twin beds. She sleep in one bed and he sleep in the other bed, you know, and when he, before he gets up in the morning she better have on her makeup, 'cause he can't stand her without no makeup, you know. She gets up in the morning now putting on her shit, you know, getting all dressed up just for him to wake up. And the first thing he say is "Where's my breakfast?" or "Where's my money?" or something, you know, and if she don't have it, then that's an ass-kicking.

According to The Book, the pimp should establish separate residences for his hos, and maintain separate accommodation for himself. But this rule was most often honored in the breach. Many variations of household composition exist.

Iceberg Slim had nothing but distain for the current trend in households, which he contrasted to the old days in Chicago when pimps and hos rigorously maintained separate apartments:

ICEBERG SLIM: Pimps had class, man. They had class! Some of them today, man, sleep with broads in... in *communes!* Like they got three girls, to save money they might have an apartment with three broads and... Man, you can't have class and pimp with class and have that sort of situation. That's not an elegant way to pimp. You can't have style - and grace - and surround yourself with an aura of godlike qualities. If you can touch God whenever you like, pretty soon you'll find out that he isn't God. He won't be a riddle any more.

In addition, problems of jealousy and competition among the women are intensified by living closely together and by allowing children to enter the picture. Several informants agree that "children are a hang-up" in The Life. There are really no rules or traditions about how they should be handled, and so each man makes up his own. Some openly raise their children in the rules of The Life, while others carefully shield their children from it. Often children get passed around from relative to near-relative, and may only stay with their mothers for short periods.

The following is an example from our field notes of a household beset with problems of children, competition between women, jealousy, and cramped living conditions. The household is headed by Mitchell, a tall, husky, and very dark man who left his native Louisiana when he was thirteen and began his pimping at the age of seventeen, when he met his main lady, Shannon. They turned out together; that is, they both decided simultaneously to enter The Life. He is a good trumpet player, and has spent more than five years seriously trying to get a foothold in the musical entertainment world, playing trumpet alone and with groups in various small soul music nightclubs. His clothing is in the mode of a black stage performer: extremely colorful, flash and dramatic. Mitchell's two white ladies are blood sisters who are both utterly devoted to him, though not always to each other. From time to time there are one to two more women in the stable. He rules them all firmly, sometimes with generous helpings of physical punishment. They live communally, and always seem to be in financial difficulty. Nevertheless, the women's devotion to Mitchell and his musical goals is genuine, moving, and somewhat infectious.

Shannon, who is the "bottom bitch" of Mitchell's stable, complained of her problems with Lana, who is their pimp's "number-two lady." She complained that her sister is taking advantage of their blood relationship, and is chippying with Mitchell while Shannon is out working.

Lana had produced him a son whom Shannon was taking care of, they were all taking care of. But since Shannon hadn't been able to have a child by Mitchell, she was put into a position of tension and competition with her blood sister, despite the fact that Shannon is supposed to be bottom woman. Her greatest sorrow is that she and Mitchell can't have a child (their Rh factors are incompatible) and she envies her sister who has "material security" by having borne their man's child.

Shannon has gotten into an argument with Mitchell after reading in Iceberg Slim's book how he kept two ladies together in one place, two other ladies together in another place, and maintained a separate apartment for himself. She was trying to convince him that that was the way they should do it; that they shouldn't all be living together because it makes for too much friction. Shannon does not have a problem of jealousy or competitiveness with the other girls, who bow to her status, but it appears that her sister Lana refuses to recognize her as bottom woman because she has a child by Mitchell and Shannon doesn't.

A pimp has to weigh carefully the economic advantages of saving rent by living together against the psychological advantages of living separately. When the stable and the pimp dwell together, there is greater larceny and competitiveness for sex on the part of the women. These two problems are related, since by stealing money from each other to give to the man, they are really vying for the position of sexual favorite. In addition, there may be other sources of stress, such as Shannon's problem over motherhood of the baby. On the other hand, if he keeps the women apart, it is more difficult for the pimp to be sure he is getting all the money, and commuting may place additional burdens upon him.

Avoiding the giant white foot

Within the subculture of The Life, we observed an even higher degree of paranoia, which we call the "Player's Norm." Fear and uncertainty are much greater among players and other hustlers than among square Blacks, but this Player's Norm is also an undeniably realistic attitude. When we interviewed Iceberg Slim in his Los Angeles home, he began by expressing his delight that in his present square existence, he no longer was fearful of a knock at the door:

ICEBERG SLIM: I'm ecstatic that I escaped the idiot's paradise. Really. When you knocked on the door? I wasn't leaping out of my skin to hide some dope. My heart wasn't palpitating. I didn't even have to peep through the blinds. I went right to the door. Look, for a roller [policeman] to come to this door –he's insane, he's gotta be a nut. Because I'm not doing anything, you dig it?

I used to live in absolute terror. Used to be afraid of having visitors, for instance. Like you have come. Well, I still don't like many visitors, even now. See, I knew a fellow named Pretty Willy, a pimp. I knew this man for thirty years. He visited me *once;* by accident I cracked [let slip] where I lived. By accident! All my friends, Baby Frank, Yo-Yo, I always met them [only] in the street.

You can miss all the rungs going down

Aside from the chance of getting caught, "fucking up," or blowing his women, the pimp game has its own natural limits.

What, we asked Iceberg Slim, is the greatest threat to a good pimp? He replied:

ICEBERG SLIM: The passage of time: you become more insecure the older you get, just like a whore becomes more insecure. That's the worst thing, the most traumatic thing about pimpin' and hoing. 'Cause you got these little fellows coming up all the time, nipping at your heels, at your broads. But you always got to have young broads to get money.

But you're getting older; older and older. You gotta have nineteen and twenty-year old broads to get money. And here you are pushing thirty-five, you got a broad, and here comes a little fellow twenty years old, "talkin' that talk and walkin' that walk" and looking the way *you* used to look with their freshness and their verve and their vitality, and you haven't GOT it. And their sweetness and lightness of heart and their charm.

Notes and references

Iceberg Slim's *Pimp* contains an extensive glossary of ghetto terms used in his book. Although there is considerable overlap with modern usage, many of the terms were peculiar to the Chicago ghetto thirty years ago, and we did not encounter them among our informants (for example "bell," notoriety connected with one's name; "crumb crusher," a baby; "yeasting," to build up or exaggerate, etc.). From Mr. Milton Van Sickle, formerly with Holloway House, we learned that Iceberg had not originally planned to include a glossary in his novel, but it was deemed necessary because the editor "at first couldn't tell what the hell he was talking about."

PORTRAIT OF A PIMP

By Helen Koblin

Los Angeles Free Press

Volume 9 No. 8 Issue 397

25th February 1972

Iceberg Slim is, in reality, Robert Beck, an elegantly handsome black man perhaps in his late forties or early fifties. Standing at six foot three, he is lithe and loose, resembling a man in his thirties. For the last dozen years or so, after the abandonment of his former life as a pimp, he has been dedicating his extraordinary energy and intellectual prowess to "good works."

As a retired pimp, he weaves exotic tales from his past into a tapestry that staggers the mind because it is a reality. He has had four books published to date. They are: Pimp, Mama Black Widow, Trick Baby and The Naked Soul. Pimp and Trick Baby are soon to be released as films. His works repetitively expose and vilify that portion of humanity that are the street hustlers.

In the past, he was the embodiment of what is known in street jargon as "The Life." Since the death of his mother, he has altered his life style totally. Now, married, with two children, he has been reborn a writer, a black artist with a social conscience. In addition he is an eloquent dramatic speaker who easily waxes poetic on the base topics - no simple matter.

Iceberg Slim has lectured at colleges and universities, and is well received by students everywhere. He feels he is in the process of learning, in all areas, and hopes to become a positive force in the black community.

The only perceivable vestige of his former life in which one can find fault is possibly in a vaguely condescending attitude toward women. This is revealed in the latter portion of the interview.

Torn by the guilt connected with his past, the loss of his mother, the guilt-love object who was perhaps the most powerful force in his life; he is now inspired to give back what he so brutally took. Robert Beck emerges a strange mosaic of a hideous past, an optimistic present and a prophetic future, a valuable man, whose life chronicles thirty years of history in Black America.

Koblin: Mr. Beck, are most pimps black?

Beck: I wouldn't know that. I would suspect though because of the disproportionate majority of white people that there might very well be more white pimps than black. But I would say that black pimps are the best because of the crucible in which they operate.

Koblin: Do pimps hate their whores?

Beck: Well, not necessarily consciously. The best pimps that I have known, that is the career pimps, the ones who could do twenty, maybe thirty years as a pimp, were utterly ruthless and brutal without compassion. They certainly had a basic hatred for women.

My theory is, and I can't prove it, if we are to use the criteria of utter ruthlessness as a guide, that all of them hated their mothers. Perhaps more accurately, I would say that they've never known love and affection, maternal love and affection. I've known several dozen in fact that were dumped into the trash bins when they were what? ...only four or five days old.

Koblin: You say you loved your mother in your book.

Beck: Of course, but underneath the threshold of consciousness, I know that I must have hated her, as demonstrated by my neglect of her through the years.

Koblin: Did you ever pursue any activities outside pimping?

Beck: No, when I was pimping, I was all pimp, unfortunately. I remember when I was a young pimp, and that's where the thrill is... when one is young enough and enforced enough and ill enough to want to be a pimp. That's where all the glory is, when one is playing Jehovah so to speak, and learning his craft.

Then oddly enough and disappointingly enough, when one learns to control eight or nine or ten women; then all the luster, all the glory is gone. It's much like learning to ski. One just does it automatically.

Then of course, all the clothes and diamonds and the cocaine, and the girls, it isn't really important. There is a vacuum that is filled by the joy of learning the intricacies of being a pimp. But it was the greatest letdown because I was reaching always.

Then I was thirty and looked like a teenager. I was most fortunate with all the debauchery, all of the horrible things I did to my body, I never really showed it. You see; it wasn't the face of Dorian Gray at any point.

So you see, my ruin was inherent in my preservation. I could go on and on because young girls, beautiful young girls related to me and found me fascinating because I was so terribly and devastatingly youthful looking. You see what I'm saying.

Koblin: Yes, and I could say that the same is still true.

Beck: Oh no, no! I'm a trillion now, you see, but then...

Koblin: You've been out of "the life" for about ten years now. Is that correct?

Beck: Longer, as I described in... the steel casket was the last bit. When I was apprehended for an escape thirteen or fourteen years before then... I might add a miraculous escape... one that they had no idea as to how it had been accomplished. I just vanished like a wisp of smoke. There were no bars sawed, and no screw's head busted. I just left. But I was apprehended for a bit of stupidity.

I had been convinced by a hustler, an ex-pimp, a really terribly ancient old man, who had stopped pimping. To earn his bread for sustenance, he sold whorehouse costumes. He had a list of whorehouses throughout the United States where he would go to sell his wares; you know, the little diaphanous costumes that are prerequisites for whorehouse girls to wear.

Koblin: Do you miss *"the life"*?

Beck: No, but after all, after you have been a pimp, and it's the bedrock of all male aspiration, if only in fantasy. For really what is the bedrock of all male aspiration if it isn't cunt and money? Now here the pimp, what has he got? All kinds of beautiful girls, who bring him cunt and money. Kiss and suck and love him... on the surface of course, because beneath they really pray for his ruin.

So you see how utterly poisoning and trapping it all is. Once anybody has pimped he is in trouble because this is what the male aspiration is... whether he is the president of a white corporation, of General Motors for example. It all boils down to the same thing... power.

Koblin: Did you handle mostly black women in your stable?

Beck: In the book Pimp, I do not mention any white women that I handled, but the truth was that when I was young, I was absolutely irresistible to white women. But they were brittle, absolutely brittle.

Koblin: Are you saying that they weren't marketable?

Beck: Oh, yes tremendously marketable, but they wanted to be petted and pampered. I was in the street, and I didn't have the face to do this. I was all pimp. There wasn't one scintilla of gigolo in me. I was uncompromising, absolutely uncompromising.

White women coming from the white world were fascinated with me. They had perhaps seen me in cabarets, or in Marshall Fields. Then they would smile at me and then we would talk and then they would follow me like little pastel puppies to where ever I wanted them to go, because I was sick and ill and a monster. But I was Svengali, or Rasputin, if you wish, so what could they do? But then they were introduced to the harsh reality of a sixteen-hour day with no days off...

Then there was that horrible thing of the family of whores, particularly my bottom woman who had incensed hatred for the so-called alabaster supercunt. (Bottom woman is that whore most trusted and relied upon by the pimp - the favorite in an intellectual sense.)

You know, black women have always felt overshadowed by the white woman, and justifiably so, because the economic and sociological pyramid in America has the white man at the apex, then the white woman, then the black man... and there down in that abyss of frustration and trauma is the black woman. So you see, it set up so much negative dynamism in the stable.

I was always bringing some luscious white woman into the stable and saying "Well here is Patricia; here is Diane." And tell my bottom women, "You show her!"

You see, I never went into the street and showed anybody anything. I never lived with no whores. There are bums you know that live in some house with a bunch of whores, but I always held above it... high up above them there, a perpetual puzzle like God Almighty Himself, and I sexed more with conversation than I ever did with my penis or my tongue.

Here again, I was using hypnosis and power, power. I used to laugh, when I'd see some fellow who was all tired and fatigued, and maybe he had three little girls and he was trying to sex them all physically.

Koblin: Then pimping is really a psychological adeptness?

Beck: Well, if you know how to pimp. If you're just some fellow with dimples, and your hair springs from your scalp in great voluptuous waves, and you're pretty, well then you're gonna rely on your beauty instead of your skull.

I was never the best looking, nor the best pimp. Among my contemporaries, there were fabulous people... young, black pimps, well, hybrids really, racial hybrids, who were beautiful. And I had to have an edge. My edge was always class. Even though I used drugs, I would never stay out with the pimps 'till 6 or 7 in the morning. I'd drink a quart of milk, no cocaine... you see, I was about to go to sleep.

Koblin: What about a black pimp? Isn't he primarily interested in money?

Beck: Yes, but a black pimp is so filled with hatred that he is never sweeter than the money. It is kick, kiss, kick, kiss, kick, kiss! He takes everything and gives up nothing, and women need love. I don't know anything about the anatomy of love... but I would say an element of concern and compassion would be included.

Koblin: However, when you became a pimp, didn't you have the same thing in mind as the white man... money and power?

Beck: Yes, the end result was, but…

Koblin: You mean that was not your goal?

Beck: A black young man does not have the premeditated conscious insight as does a white young man when he sets out to destroy people to become a millionaire. It is for the black man, a survival. It is a ghetto kid, deprived of fatherhood, raised by his mother who has no father either. He searches for his father image and sees Dandy Bill or Lovely Louie and these are the people in his environment whom he wants to emulate. And Dandy Bill is a pimp.

Koblin: Do you socialize with other people in the ghetto?

Beck: Oh, yes, whenever I come out, all kinds of young black studs converge upon me. Some of them are ill. They want to pick my brain for the treasures they think are buried there, like how to pimp. I always dissuade them.

Koblin: How do you prevent other young people from going into "the life?"

Beck: Well, first of all, they admire me almost universally now, in Black America. When I appear before a group of young people, white or black, they almost immediately forget the fact that I am from another generation.

I approach them this way, at San Jose State, for example: I come out and say, 'I would like to disclaim that I ain't no lecturer. I'm just a street nigger who's come here to rap with you and who's learning to be a writer.' None of the pompous stuff. Otherwise, they become disenchanted and that's why they reject just about all the men my age.

Koblin: You hate cops, I take it.

Beck: No, I pity them.

Koblin: Are they like Plato's soldiers, the lowest on the intellectual rung?

Beck: Let's put it this way. I can dig a black man becoming a cop, but what fatal flaw does this white man have that he should want to become a member of the most hated and despised society not only by black people, but also most young people.

Koblin: You said once, "There are times when you must choose sides when you are going to be a black writer." Can you explain that?

Beck: Yes, ten or fifteen years ago, a black writer would talk out of both sides of his mouth, just as so-called black leaders. They could delude and fascinate, hypnotize large segments of black people from grass roots, ordinary black street people all the way up.

Then came Martin Luther King. He started to make black people aware of the potential power they had. Then Malcolm came and defined the enemy. Black people became aware.

There was the most brilliant black writer, I do not care to mention his name, whom I idolized. Now, you talk about magnificent convolutions, God Almighty! But unfortunately, he always talked under fake fire. He was always full of fake fire.

In other words on the surface he would say things that seemed absolutely revolutionary, but when the probing mind examined it, it was pussy right down to the bone.

Koblin: Are you then in agreement with the black militants.

Beck: I'm in agreement with anybody that wants freedom, and who wants some sort of equality in this genocidal society.

Koblin: What do you think of the young black militants as personified by Huey Newton, say?

Beck: I think he's beautiful. His philosophy has just been transposed a bit. It is much more realistic, Bobby Seale just related to it this way. "We have not abandoned the gun, we have recognized the importance of the hammer to build. We must build educational facilities. We must build medical facilities. And we must keep our guns within reach to defend our right to build." And I thought that was just beautiful.

Koblin: Isn't he also a hoodlum?

Beck: Well, yes, he has been conditioned that way. But... a hoodlum poet! Oh, my God. But then, he has never suffered the way I did. You see, all of the beauty was cauterized out of me. But he is beautiful to a fault. I have never been able to write poetry. I have envied him that. But here again, he didn't suffer long enough.

Koblin: He did do time in jail...

Beck: Not long enough, though. You see, I suffered repetitively. And he was comparatively young. But anyway, I'm glad he retained this poetic thing. He is so outta sight. The man is just miraculous.

Koblin: What happened the last time you saw your mother?

Beck: [acting out his words] There she was, the wasted face framed by wild white hair. I stood there; her eyes were closed. I realized she was sleeping. I had a rose in my hand and a heart full of remorse and guilt. I sat quietly and watched her whisper. I said, "Mama" and she didn't respond. I was alarmed because I thought she had gone into a coma. She had diabetes, you see.

I said, "Mama." There was a flicker on those incredibly long eyelashes, that had just set the hearts of so many black men aswoon when she was beautiful and young and in her prime and tall and handsome and stately and utterly queenly. And then she opened those great sage voluminous eyes.

Then she looked up at me and I said "Darling (I lied), you look so much better than you did yesterday." Then her mouth tightened; that sensual, magnificent mouth of hers - and the eyes - were mean because she knew that I was being insincere.

I said, "Mama, you really do!" And she said, "I'm old and ugly; I am not a whore. Don't you try to fool me or lie to me."

"I'm gonna tell you somethin'. Mama, the reason you're so sick is because you won't forgive me, Mama, you ain't gonna live if you don't forgive me. You got to forgive me if you gonna live. And that's what's wrong. That's why you got that tight look on your mouth. You can't forgive me for what I done to you. And I'm sorry, Mama. Don't you think I remember how you carried me through the streets of Chicago when I was six months old. It was ten below zero, and you were in the very fabulous years of golden womanhood. You didn't desert me or neglect me. You were there, Mama, all the time. I'm aware of it now Mama; I really am. Now, don't you play like that with me, Mama. Now open your eyes, Mama... [voice reaches screaming pitch, weeping] Mama, Mama, Mama! You're gonna kill me, Mama. Why did you kill me, Mama?"

Koblin: Why is there an actor portraying you in Pimp and Trick Baby?

Beck: I was considered for Blue Howard, but Blue was a portly man with a stocky body. And for Pimp, they wanted someone fresh, you know. I'm well preserved now, but let's face that.

Koblin: Would you have preferred to play the part yourself?

Beck: No, not that part. I'd like to play something completely divorced from that. But I hope that I have been able to convince you that I can act, just with that little bit about Mama. And there are people down there that can outact me.

Koblin: A black nationalist stated that it is the responsibility of the black artist to destroy the glamorous image of the pimp, and his victims forever. Do you agree with that?

Beck: Yes, here again, it is counter-revolutionary for black people to prey on other black people, or upon poor white people. I recognize the necessity for crime in Black America. I understand why, for survival, black people must steal. But I don't condone crime. I feel that what it takes to be a successful criminal could be used in a more constructive way.

Like if the pimp has enough circuitry going in his brain to control nine women, surely, he's got no business being a pimp. So if you're black, and you must be a criminal, don't steal my stuff. Go over there. Steal from affluent white people.

Koblin: The black pimp, as you were, has made his fortune through the total degradation of the black woman in this society. Is that true?

Beck: That's true. And the tragedy there is, that the black woman is the bedrock of the black family unit. This is what is under direct assault. It occurred under the structured racism of America. When a black man turns out a black woman, he is denigrating the bedrock of family life in his community. Again, this is counter-revolutionary. Pimps are becoming an anachronism.

Koblin: You have then assisted in the degradation of your own race.

Beck: Yes, before I got insight.

Koblin: Do black men consciously or unconsciously hate white women now?

Beck: They have mixed feelings. After all, possession of the white woman must evoke images of lynchings, the victims with their balls hacked off, their throats cut, swinging from Georgia peach trees.

On the other hand, the black man as well as the white, has been conditioned to believe that the white woman is superior to all other women. The alabaster supercunt has always held dominion in the aesthetic caste system as perpetuated by our mass media. Some white women marry black men, but these unions have a high mortality rate.

Koblin: Marilyn Monroe was a supercunt in our society, and we are aware of her tragedy. Is she on the same psychological strata in our society as the black male supercock?

Beck: Yes.

Koblin: Do white women suffer the same oppression as black men?

Beck: Yes, she is overshadowed by the white man also. The white man still remains at the apex of the pyramid to which he arrived at his base nature, his brutal, psychotic ego. That's why they hate him now. They want to cut his throat.

Koblin: Who are "they?"

Beck: All of the people beneath him, in varying degrees.

Koblin: What do you think of the feminist revolution that is going on now? ...predominantly white.

Beck: You mean the lib thing? I think it is a minimal irritant. But it is good, it is a distraction to the giant. While his toes are being stepped on, you can rape him with an iron pipe.

Koblin: What is it that a woman wants in a man?

Beck: All women want to possess a man and not share him. It is a primeval biological need. If this need is not satisfied, she builds a desire to avenge herself.

"ICEBERG SLIM" PORTRAYS GRIM LIFE

By Fred Dickey

San Jose Mercury-News

30th April 1972

The nicest thing one can say about Robert Beck – or any other writer, for that matter – is that what you read is what he is. Beck, known by his pen name of Iceberg Slim, is the black ex-Chicago pimp who quit his occupation and drug habit and turned writer.

But I make it sound too pat. Robert Beck didn't just turn writer, he became a searching and searing black voice trumpeting from the ghetto darkness.

In his books, "Pimp: The Story of My Life," "Trick Baby," "Mama Black Widow," and "The Naked Soul of Iceberg Slim," (all published by Holloway House) he has captured the humor, excitement and danger of ghetto existence without loosing its most essential ingredient – sordidness. His writing has authored one of the most remarkable success stories in modern American literature. Beck's books have sold the astounding total of 2,000,000 copies. Plans are being made to make movies of "Pimp…" and "Trick Baby."

Success itself is not an unknown thing to 52-year-old Beck, but the polite, respectable variety and he were strangers until 12 years ago. Then, after several months in solitary confinement in a Chicago jail during which he barley managed to survive and keep his sanity, Beck got his head straight due mainly to the death of his mother, which shocked him awake, kicked his heroin habit, "cold turkey," and was ready for the straight world which immediately let it be known that it wasn't ready for Iceberg Slim. Every place where he applied for work immediately took the sign out of the window.

What the employers didn't realize was that they weren't denying just a 40ish, unemployed, inexperienced Negro; they were rejecting an artist, a learned practitioner, of the ancient craft of procuring. Beck didn't list his former calling on his resume, but he knew, as have so many frustrated blacks before him, of his essential intelligence, cunning and ability to influence and control others. He was a helluva pimp.

Spurned as a 9-to-5er by the business world, he turned to writing with astounding success.

They didn't call him Iceberg for nothing. Inscrutable. Cold as ice...

"A pimp is a substitute love object for a whore. He's got to be god to her, and god can't laugh, show weakness or be human. If he does, he looses the whore to a better pimp."

"What he has to do," the tall, angular Beck explains, "is to construct an air castle for her." Failing that, sometimes a beating with a straightened wire coat hangar, as Beck admits to having done, will make her fall into line.

If he does all of that successfully the pimp will "turn out" many whores and have "his game uptight," Beck explains in the language of the ghetto.

Looking backward, Beck views the black pimp as an object of pity. Crushed in the crucible of bigotry with no realistic means of attaining his potential, of realizing his manhood, the clever, ambitious black youth turns to the one product that enough white men are always willing to buy – black women. Before the dawning of black consciousness, the pimp didn't realize – or care – that he was fattening on the flesh of his own people.

This is a seamy side of black existence that Beck feels must be described as a distinct social phenomenon. He resents the "respectable" black writers who would like to pretend such things never existed and who scorn his efforts to portray the life of a "street nigger."

Beck sees and interprets signs of hope. He takes pleasure in the rise of the black militancy because he sees it as a constructive outlet for the pride and drive of today's young blacks therefore largely replacing crime as a release for frustration and pent-up ambitions.

Beck takes particular delight that young black girls are increasingly receiving new alternatives to prostitution. Every ghetto girl who goes to business school and becomes a secretary, lessens the stockpile from which the pimp must draw, he explains.

Robert Beck has no illusions about his past and grieves over the pain he's inflicted. But though he has shorn the old existences and now lives the middle-class life with his wife and four children in Los Angeles, he refuses to act pious.

"Don't say I've reformed: that's too esoteric. Just say I'm a retired pimp."

Then, he says, steadily and confidently, "My life's been sick; but I'm not as sick as I was and I'm getting better all the time."

Bob Beck, Iceberg Slim, has been places that shouldn't be allowed to exist and he's done things that people shouldn't be allowed to do, but because they do and he did, his telling us about them fulfills an important literary function.

"Time had scissored away my hair in front. I didn't look much like the mug shot of that sleek escapee."
Pimp: the Story of My Life

Circa 1967-1971. Publisher's publicity photo. Courtesy Holloway House Publishing Co., Los Angeles, CA.

PIMPS ARE CHARMING CON MEN WHO HATE WOMEN: ICEBERG SLIM

By Les Matthews

New York Amsterdam News

3rd February 1973

"A pimp cannot allow himself to fall in love with a woman. He must be well groomed, well read and has to be an amateur psychiatrist." according to the author of "Trick Baby" which opened last Friday with Kiel Martin and Mel Stewart co-starring.

The author, "Iceberg Slim" whose name is Robert Beck, said he received his education in prison where he did four stretches. "I read everything in prison. I became educated and while doing time in prison I became a changed man." he said.

"Iceberg Slim" who was brought up on South Side became a pimp and a con man because the handsome boys he grew up with were in the business and doing well. He would watch the older pimps and pattern himself after them. Soon they were calling him "Youngblood."

"One afternoon I was standing in front of a bar and two men were having a heated discussion. I had taken some cocaine and was counting bubbles in my glass which was filled with Seven Up. One of the men arguing took a gun out of his pocket and fired several shots at his friend killing him. One of the bullets went through my hat. I took the hat off and said 'If I had a pointed head I would be in trouble.'"

"A friend who was known as 'Glasstop' heard me and walked over to me and said you're cold just like an iceberg. I'm going to call you Iceberg Slim and that's how I got my name." he said.

"Pimps, years ago, were different from the pimps of today. The men years ago were suave, well dressed and they had a luxurious pad. The pimp of years gone were students of human nature. They would hypnotise some women or bewitch them with their charm.

I learned to use intrigue and control the minds of women from older pimps. The pimps years ago had a bad habit and that was beating their women which would damage the merchandise. Today a number of pimps use dope to control their women. I don't call them pimps. The dope is the pimp and they are scavengers." he said.

Iceberg Slim who doesn't smoke or drink said he gave up pimping and conning people out of their money when he was 43. "I found out that old pimps are used by the whores and some become kept men. I was a monster and I couldn't allow myself to be reduced to a gigolo. I learned my craft. I seduced women. I was their master and I enjoy living high. Pimps are lousy lovers." he said.

"I am a happy man today. I enjoy writing books, lecturing to colleges and schools. I enjoy my wife, Catherine Betty, whom I married ten years ago and our three daughters Camille, Bellissa, Melody and our son Junior. I don't want a pimp trying to turn out my daughter but I will have them well schooled about the sordid life of a pimp, whore and con men and women.

It's a life I wouldn't recommend to my worst enemy. Today I am a better man because of my background; but knowing about it I wouldn't do it over again." Dig "Trick Baby" at the DeMille Theatre. You will have a ball!

Why the pseudonym of Iceberg? "Iceberg," says the writer, "is a descriptive picture of what the real hustler epitomizes. I 'squared up' and changed my life-style when I was 40 years old – an elderly age for a man living outside the law. I had the chance, in prison, to examine my conscience and there was my overwhelming guilt, as well as realization that I had wasted so many years. I had much to atone for."

The sole quote from Iceberg in Universal's press pack for Trick Baby, 1973.

IT WASN'T MORAL INSIGHT, HE WAS JUST GROWING OLDER

The transformation of Iceberg Slim

By David Shear

Philadelphia Bulletin

4th February 1973

"My life has been rich in the kinds of things that audiences want to hear, I certainly wouldn't be the student of human nature that I am if I had been a 9 to 5 guy" Iceberg Slim.

AUTHOR ICEBERG SLIM (real name Robert Beck) certainly has not led a sedate life. He was a pimp in Chicago for 25 years, served four prison terms for a total of seven years and had a drug habit for nine years. Eleven years ago he left the underworld and went straight. After a variety of jobs, he sold his first novel in 1967, wrote three more, and is currently touring the country promoting the film version of his "Trick Baby."

Beck, now in his fifties, is a commanding figure, a Svengali-like presence with a mannered, almost-pompous-way-of-speaking. During the first part of a luncheon interview at the Warwick, he virtually interviewed himself, asking himself questions he thought the interviewer would ask. He eventually became more relaxed and less formal.

He characterized his life as a pimp as a "roundelay of curvaceous, uninhibited females and the finest drugs."

"Pimps," he explained, "like aging prize-fighters, loose their reactions. In the case of the pimp, it's his mental reactions that usually go. His mental reactions become dulled by insecurity. One of the important motive forces that propels the pimp forward is self confidence, almost psychotic self confidence. When there is a substantial erosion of self confidence in the pimp, he projects it, and the girls he interviews – potential victims – they sense it, and he is then not as potent. He finds difficulty gaining control of them."

"I was forced out of pimping. It wasn't that I had developed some moral insight or that I had suddenly become religious. It was the hard reality that I was older. I had seen

71

older men who stayed in the game too long, trying to support their habits, and how difficult it was, and how shabbily the prostitutes treated them. I didn't want that to happen to me."

Beck was interrupted from time to time during his recollections by women modelling dresses and rings available at the Warwick. It's doubtful if they realized the conversation dealt with a world far removed from the fashion shows and lengthy lunches.

He knew that if he left pimping, he'd have to commit five felonies every 24 hours to support both his drug habit ("a terrible trap") and life style. When he was younger, he'd been schooled by a fellow prisoner in how to "do time" – no correspondence or visits from women, no calendars, lots of reading – but at age of 41 he had a wife and four children and roots, and he didn't think he'd be able to shut them out.

"I had a fear of prison and I didn't want to be a dupe or playtoy of young prostitutes – I didn't want to be ludicrous and pathetic." He recalled.

So this self-professed "voluptuary" made "a relatively simple transfer. The same integrity that I had in the underworld I've brought to this other world, I'm a responsible husband and father because when I was in the underworld I was a responsible predator."

This erstwhile "predator" saw a newspaper ad in 1967 soliciting manuscripts. He submitted a 50-page outline which eventually became the novel "Pimp: The Story of My Life."

"Trick Baby" followed. It's the story of two black con men (Blue Howard and White Folks, who had a white father) and their various exploits. Beck, who knew the actual characters while in prison, expected the worst from the film version.

He and his wife went to a screening of the movie, which was shot in Philadelphia. "I told my wife, 'Let's keep our coats on. If the predictable happens, let's just walk out. Let's show our distain.' Do you know, we sat there with our overcoats on, sweltering. Mel Stewart made Blue Howard come alive for me. It was electrifying to see how well done the film was." Beck said, citing its under $300,000 budget.

Subsequently, Beck has had meetings with the film's distributor, Universal, to discuss an original screenplay and the filming of "Pimp."

SWEET TALK, HUSTLE AND MUSCLE

By Hollie I West

The Washington Post

1973

A player's handle is like a coded message of his élan, skills and aspirations - be he pimp, con man, or gambler. In a world where style is more important than content, the absence of a picturesque nom de guerre is equivalent to a pimp losing his righteous swagger and affecting the walk of a bank clerk.

So if you're known as Iceberg Slim, you can parlay your name into double trouble for the squares and whores. "The best pimps," he has written, "keep a steel lid on their emotions and I was one of the iciest."

Iceberg Slim, 6-foot-3, 180 pounds, broad-shouldered and the best known pimp of our time, played God for women all over the Midwest, mostly in Chicago, from the late 1930's to about 1961.

Sweet talk and psychology were his main game. His aim was to look through the head of a whore and read her thoughts. If persuasion didn't work he turned to violence. His prime bit was to roll up two coat hangers into a truncheon and flail women's naked backs until they bent to his will. In his leisure, he sniffed coke, shot heroin and drank good Scotch.

Iceberg Slim started pimping at age 18 and quit at 42. In between he controlled hundreds of women, lived high and fine and served seven years in jail, including stretches at Leavenworth, the Cook County House of Corrections and Waupan State Prison in Wisconsin.

Now that he's out of "The Life" he is exploring what drove him to brutalize and dehumanize women - and himself.

He chronicles all this in volleys of prose in *Pimp: the Story of My Life*, which has sailed through 19 printings and sold more than 1.75 million copies, mostly to young blacks. Iceberg Slim may have done for the pimp what Jean Genet did for the homosexual and thief: articulate the thoughts and feelings of someone who's been there.

The Iceberg Slim of yesteryear is considered an anachronism to the young dudes now out there on the block trying to hustle. They say he is crude and violent, overlooking his staggering gift of gab. Iceberg acknowledges that pimping has changed because "women have changed." The advent of women's lib, changing sexual mores, general affluence in this society and widespread use of drugs by pimps to control prostitutes have made an impact.

Getting right down to it, however, pimping is still basically sweet talk and looking pretty. But psychology has its limits. When whores tire of it, as pointed out in *Black Players*, the anthropological study of pimps in San Francisco, young pimps still use muscle.

Iceberg Slim was born Aug. 4, 1918, in Chicago, and lived much of his childhood in Milwaukee and Rockford, Ill. before returning to Chicago as a teenager. His father deserted the family when Iceberg was a child. His mother, whom he says helped pave the way for him becoming a pimp by pampering him, supported the two of them by working as a domestic and operating a beauty parlor - all the while being exploited herself by vagabond men.

Iceberg attended Tuskegee Institute briefly in the mid-1930's, at the same time Ralph Ellison was there (they did not know each other).

The Iceberg Slim of today is noticeably toned down from the high liver of yesterday. He is known as Bob or Robert Beck, his true name. He has been a steady family man for 12 years and has four children, ranging in age from 2 to 10.

He spends most of his time writing at his home in Los Angeles, but also lectures at high schools and colleges about the degradation of street life: hustling, drug-dealing and pimping.

His books are all drawn from personal experience. *Trick Baby*, the biography of a con man has just been released in movie form and is playing at Loew's Palace and Republic theaters; *Mama Black Widow* is the story of a homosexual queen and *The Naked Soul Of Iceberg Slim* is a collection of essays. He is currently working on a novel about an Italian gangland enforcer.

Holloway House, Iceberg Slim's publisher, says his books have sold in excess of 3.5 million in bookstores of all types: those along burlesque strips and in suburban areas. Officials at Brentano's say their F Street store has had difficulty keeping *Pimp* on its shelves for the last two years. They also say his books sell well at branch stores in Chevy Chase and Hyattsville.

Iceberg Slim was in Washington, DC recently. Here are excerpts from a conversation with this reporter:

Q: What was your main hustle when you were at your peak?

A: Ressin' and dressin'. I just rested and dressed. And petted my dog and ate chocolates and slept on satin sheets. And went to the penitentiary periodically, I might add. It was interesting - to survive it and still be able to make sense. After all, I talked to a fellow who was the brightest among us. I can't call his name. And the last time I saw him about a year and a half ago, I didn't know what he was talking about. He was almost gibberish. His brain was shot - the circuitry was gone. He was so fast, man, in his prime. He just vibrated. He'd had a heart attack. That was when I realized I hadn't missed anything in squaring up. And when I came back to Chicago a year and a half ago for the first time in 11 years I wondered what had fascinated me, man. This shows you what happened to me in California, right - something aside from the transition from that to writing happened. It had to, man, if I'm viewing Chicago as a place of great ugliness when I used to even love the clouds of dirt that fell.

Q: In the book *Pimp* you wrote that you were "almost certain that the principles of good pimping apply to all man-and-woman relationships." Will you expand on that?

A: What I was saying was that the pimp overtly and almost without inhibition, denigrates and despoils the sexual object. His mauling of the sexual object is perhaps a more severe version of what happens in conventional relationships. For instance, in so-called "square" sexual bouts, the woman winds up, of course, flat on her back in a submissive position. If a man is aware of what sexual button to push to enhance a woman's gratification, he will bite her with the proper degree of ferocity. If he inflicted that kind of punishment on her when she was not in a state of rapture, she would resent it... The kiss-kick ritual is at the very root of the pimp's sexuality. My theory is that some quantum of pimp in every man would perhaps enhance his approach to women, because I think it's a truism that women gravitate to a man who can at least flash transient evidence of heelism. I think that the angelic, completely pure paragon, is not too interesting. Women are prone to masochism, anyway. I think if you are able to manufacture a bit of "heelism" in your nature and give them a sense of insecurity as to whether some voluptuous rival might come along and steal you, then you are a treasured jewel. I think women are it. It's the concept of the pimp who has one whore, who'll create a competitive situation to gadfly the one whore he's got, will manufacture and create the illusion that he has another whore who's sending him money orders from some whorehouse upstate. And he will ecstatically unfurl the money order, which, ironically, is the money that the one whore has made.

Q: Of all the pimps, you have been the only one who has written extensively about your experiences. What prompted you to write?

A: Nothing prompted me. First of all, I am of superior intelligence. We start with that premise. If we start with the subsidiary premise that I have a family, and because I am my age and they are infants, I have to make a necessary imprint. If you don't make an imprint you aren't going to be able to get large sums of money. That's absolutely if you're a nigger. You've got to be spectacular and transcendental - otherwise you ain't gonna get a whole lot of bread.

If I were alone, If I didn't have three beautiful daughters, I could just rest on my laurels and just sit at home and live off $12,000 or $15,000 a year, and that would be the end of it. But I know that I can't do that. I know that I've got to find some way to make the kind of imprint that will get me very quickly large sums of money so that I could put the proper cushioning under my children. So that if I should pass away suddenly, then I have made arrangements for my three daughters and my son. But most of all I should like to prove to the world, to dispel the myth that street niggers are devoid of intellect. You know that's a myth. They think we are devoid of wit. I want to prove to older black men, just because you're past age 50, man, don't give up.

Q: How did you learn to write?

A: Can you imagine when you're 55 how desperately - since you've been removed from that ferocious competition that is pimping - you would bring the same drives to this other world. I've always been a creature of pressure. My wife is 20 years younger than I. She represents another gadfly. It's no one particular thing but rather a number of things - a man married to a woman 20 years younger, infant children, displaced pimp, 55. I've got to try.

Q: As a rule, pimps find it practical to be distant in their relations with women. In fact, your trade name derives from your icy nature. Have you been able to warm up to your wife and children?

A: Yes, but with my wife there's a difference. She's been with me for more than 11 years. Do you understand how horrible it would be for Iceberg Slim to be with a woman who wasn't with him from the beginning - when Iceberg Slim was fresh out of prison. This woman was with me when I ain't had two red quarters to put together.

Now my ambition is to be as good as a father as I was a pimp. But at first I couldn't express love for my daughters because they were female. I can do it now. But you know what pulled my coat. You know how balmy the weather is in L.A., right. There are scores of fathers - black and white - with the supermarket syndrome. They ride their kids in carts. And you see fathers in California doing the shopping and all. When I first saw it, man - these fathers kissing their children, fondling them - I just looked and said to myself, 'That nigger is a shonuff father.' I know I wasn't so sick that I couldn't realize that he knew what to do, or that he wasn't flawed.

So that's what woke me up to the fact that something was wrong with me. I would stand off from all my children and I had a morbid fear of being kissed by them. When you're a pimp, you're only as sweet as the money. They were like little whores and I'd say, 'Now get out of here.' They would giggle and laugh at me. That's bad medicine for a kid, you understand what I mean. The rationale was 'they like that,' I'd tell the old lady. She'd just look at me. She'd say, 'They ain't gonna understand their daddy.'

Now I had a habit - just to show you how erudite my old lady is - of picking up my kids with their back toward me. She said, 'Daddy, dear, they can't feel secure in that position. Don't hold them with their backs to you. The supporting thing isn't there.' I would say to myself, 'Of course she's right. There ain't no support - no security there.' Ain't that a bitch - I didn't know that, slick as I try to be.

Q: Why did you get out of pimping?

A: I got out of it because I was old. I did not want to be teased, tormented and brutalized by young whores. And there were too many young dudes, dressing well, looking pretty and talking good - to these young whores.

Q: What was your next step?

A: Ringing doorbells and selling insecticide.

Q: You were quoted in the book *Black Players* as saying you were "ecstatic" about leaving the life.

A: Oooooow, God! I leave the door open in hotel rooms. I take the chain and put it so the door can't lock and I might take a nap. I don't have to worry because I ain't stupid enough like old pimps to have that gangster grass or any other contraband with me as I travel. I ain't worried about no rollers [police detectives]. I ain't gonna do nothing wrong. Ain't no way they can indict me for anything. I don't even entertain women. I don't have no sexual contact with women.

Q: Has pimping changed since you quit?

A: Pimping has to change, man, because you see, women changed. With the advent of television young girls could see the opulence of the inside of star's homes. The girl would see authentic opulence. Then when the pimp would take them to these bares [empty apartments]. A pimp would buy yard goods. He'd have his bottom woman go down and get satin by the bolt. He would take sometimes tacks and cover a wall with satin, so there was only a kind of sleazy opulence. So when the pimp would take these young girls, who had already seen true opulence via the boob tube, it didn't have the true impact he wanted. She was not aswoon at this synthetic splendor.

And there was a proliferation of luxury cars with the end of the war (World War II). Shoeshiners had Cadillacs. They might've been selling a little gangster on the side, but they still had Cadillacs. Where formerly only pimps and high powered gamblers and numbers bankers had these luxury cars, there was just a proliferation of them. No young girl is titillated because she sees a new Eldorado. She isn't stunned or hypnotized as she once was when some dude would pull up in one of them long Caddies.

These are some of the things that happened. Maybe this is why large numbers of pimps started using the more potent means of persuasion and treatment and recruitment, like getting the whores hooked on hard stuff, because it it a sure shot. It was the muting of the impact of what was formerly potent.

So the young pimp's reached the point where he now uses heroin as his principle weapon as he's evolved into this negative position.

Q: Isn't a woman useless if she's on drugs.

A: If she's 17, 18, or 19, and if she's supplied with drugs that are relatively good - in other words you don't have two and three percent stuff - she ain't going to get sick. You know what's bad about drug addiction. Man, it ain't the drugs that you shoot - it's if you are a hustler and if you have to hustle or steal or do whatever that you do when you're sick. And you go for X number of hours and be under stress and tension of trying to tilt that or pick a pocket, and you're sicker than a motherfucker. Then you multiply these various times when you are sick - this is what pulls you down.

That's what's wrong about drugs, but I never say this, of course. I don't want to give anybody the impression that it's therapeutic. I never looked like I had a habit. You couldn't tell I had a habit unless you were a roller [detective] and examined me. Then you could tell because it's like embalming fluid. That's the proper parallel. You just have to keep lots of it in the corpse. That's what you are.

Q: Why do you think there are so few white pimps?

A: Because there's so many other areas of chicanery, which are much more lucrative, that are open to white fellows. White men who have those instincts that would lead them to pimping prey on rich widows and there're literally just hundreds of thousands of them who have enough money that makes them a worthwhile target. So the pernicious white man, instead of pimping, shoots for one mark, one victim and he takes that broad and spends it on flashy young broads and makes the Vegas scene. If he's really a top-notcher, he makes the French Riviera. They are called 'players.' Most white guys became players because they've got the prey. They don't really have to come down to street level to get their bread. White widows with $80,000 or $90,000 are not uncommon. They don't even cause a social ripple. You know - some white woman with $90,000 - she ain't got no money according to this country's standards. If a black widow or a black woman has $90,000, man, my God - she's rich. You know these food places that are really busy like barbecue joints where they give you a ticket. Well, that's what she'd have to do. She'd have to interview niggers because they'd be playing for that 90 grand. Here again the same old opportunity and plethora of opportunity. Who wants to pimp? Why would a personable, attractive young white guy have to get down on the street level? It ain't worth it if you're white. All right, so you're getting a grand a week from all three girls - that's $3,000 a week. Then you got your nut - the police. All of the convoluted thinking that it takes just to keep a stable together and move from one posh watering and feeding spot to another and rip 'em off.

Large numbers of white pimps just have not had to do that raunchy kind of hustling that the black pimp must do. You know, there're droves of young niggers who want to pimp just to get an Eldorado, and that doesn't require a hell of a lot as you know. I mean if you can somehow get together $2,000 or $3,000 you can put a ride on the street - an Eldorado. But white guys shoot for larger goals, and most white hustlers are better educated than the average street-aspired black hustler. They just don't have to stoop.

Q: You said in the preface to your autobiography that you aim was to save youngsters from the same kind of life you lived. Have you?

A: No. They rationalize. They think they'd be slicker than I. It's almost impossible to dissuade young dudes who're already street poisoned because almost without exception they have no recourse but to think they're slicker than Iceberg. They think I'm some sort of anachronism.

THE PSYCHOLOGY OF THE PIMP

Iceberg Slim Reveals the Reality

By Kalamu ya Salaam

The Black Collegian

January/February 1975

ICEBERG SLIM is the name most commonly associated with pimps. His book PIMP: STORY OF MY LIFE is considered the number one pimp book. Robert Beck no longer pimps, for him Iceberg Slim is part of the past. However as a writer and lecturer he travels from place to place making use of his past experiences to attempt to discourage young people from pursuing the kind of life he once lived. His observations of the psychology of the pimp are revealing analyzations of what has been recently glamorized as a "boss occupation." Other books by Mr. Beck are TRICK BABY, MAMA BLACK WIDOW and THE NAKED SOUL OF ICEBERG SLIM.

BLACK COLLEGIAN: What do you see as your purpose in life now?

SLIM: My purpose is twofold. I'm 57 years old. I don't have to tell you about the psychological state of those black people that have survived past 50 in this country. Most of them have a depressed, almost fatalistic feeling of frustration as if there's no hope. All their dreams for the most part have been unrealized. As you know we all must have some sense of importance. One of the terrible by-products of the structure of racism in America is that it robs disadvantaged people, whether black, white, Chicano, of this very valuable human feeling of satisfaction.

I hope that the trip I've taken from the terrible of the pimping, the dope, and the penitentiary and diabetes to my present condition might be some sort of inspiration.

With the young people, that's purely a selfish motive. It keeps me young when they're interested in me. You might say I'm a kind of sociological vampire. I feed upon this youth, their enthusiasm. It keeps me young. But of course, it's a benign vampire act. Hopefully I can turn some of them away from the kind of trap I fell pray to.

BLACK COLLEGIAN: What kind of trap did you fall prey to?

SLIM: First of all, I fell prey to the visual trap of "pimp trappins" at an early age, when I was at my most impressionable age. This is what leads to street poisoning. If you're very young, you see some dude with spectacular clothes, the bad ride and so forth and so on and we want that. But we don't realize the misery and trauma that's behind that. It looks so good and so easy but it really isn't. It's a trap. You'd be better off with no money, just crashing here and there, sleeping where you can.

BLACK COLLEGIAN: Do you see many of those trappings in society today?

SLIM: Oh yes.

BLACK COLLEGIAN: Are the trappings the same way as when you came up?

SLIM: Yes, but they don't have the same affect on me now.

BLACK COLLEGIAN: What were some of the other trappings that attracted you?

SLIM: Jewels. The kind that coruscated in the sun when I was a boy, particularly those that coruscated in the mouth because it was the vogue back in those days. The top echelon pimps used to implant diamonds in their teeth. But pimping is not all flash.

You know there are some people who would like to believe that I am a monster in perpetuity, that I haven't really reformed. But in any case let me give you some idea of the horror in a pimp's wake. I was 22 years old. All of the black pimps from all over the country had gravitated to Detroit. The town was "open" and the news flashes across the country when a town is open.

BLACK COLLEGIAN: What do you mean?

SLIM: That means that you can work the town. You can pay off and the police will cut you loose if you get busted. The town was open. It closed after about a year. After it closed you got stringent sentences and all of the rest of that. I had been able to get a stable of six during that year. When I went there I only had one girl. So I heard that Lima, Ohio was open and good even though it was smaller. So now we're going to start the trek. In those days you worked your stable to your next destination. In other words if you stopped in town, the pimp would put the stable down in the street and then he'd go to bed. One of the secrets of longevity as a pimp is to keep yourself rested and soft looking as a young pimp because that's what pays off. If you don't have the pampered look you can't get any money.

So I stopped in Akron, Ohio, the rubber capital and I put the stable down in custody of my "bottom woman." Among those six girls was a beautiful "café au lait." I got her about three weeks before I left Detroit. We were traveling in two Cadillacs and on the way she complained, not too much though, she said "Daddy, I must have some indigestion." We had stopped to get some sandwiches or something. I said "I told you about wolfing your food down." I figured it was indigestion. So when we got in, I got a suite and they got a suite. I gave my "bottom woman" instructions. I had a chart on every town where there could be some money made. I knew just how to work a town and what instructions to give, what streets and what areas to work. So after I gave my "bottom woman" her instructions, I gave the whole stable instructions. They went on and got down.

In about an hour my "bottom woman" came and she said Leander's perspiring and she's weak and sitting on the curb out there complaining of pains. So I said "WHEN DID YOU GET TO BE MY MEDICAL SPECIALIST BITCH?"

That shows you about the monster within, when you pimp. If you're not that way, you can't pimp. You're forced into that because the pimp who trained you trained you that way. On those fast tracks there ain't no money unless you know how to pimp. There's no way that you can get money if you don't know and if you don't say the right thing at the right time. You can't have no heart. If you bring heart into it, forget it. As this hardens, your psyche hardens; you get crazier, and crazier. Then you start using cocaine and banging dope directly into the veins. Then your heart is encased in ice and if you are motivated by unconscious "mother-hatred" then you got it. Most of the pimps that I knew, I'm talking about the all-time monsters in the east, have been fellows who were never given love and affection by their mothers. It's my theory that the bestial pimps are the ones who have never known love and affection.

So I said to my "bottom woman," "Get back out in the street, get that whore up and walking and whore working."

Now every pimp I've ever known, even though he was a thorough monster to the human beings under his control, had a pet. He always had a dog or something. Some of them had lions and cubs. I know niggers that had panthers, as babies and when they'd get large they'd get another one, and even bears. They would kiss these animals right on the muzzle and just sleep with them, embrace them, buy them the finest food. If the animal got cold, they'd get up and throw an overcoat over their pajamas to get the vet. That's human right?

I know a pimp that killed a man that ran over his dog. That shows you the displaced humanism. It isn't that the pimp isn't human. He simply diverts his humanity from a woman and seeks substitute gratification in the form of a dog and so forth.

Now, back to the vignette. About an hour and a half later here she comes again. This is unprecedented. She's a field marshal. The "bottom woman" is supposed to keep pressure off the pimp so he can get his rest. That's why in L.A. you see pimps running up and down the streets in their Eldorados, it's because they don't have a "bottom woman." Looking and getting their bread and sitting and parking and staking out. They haven't got a "bottom woman." When they get 35 they'll look like they're 70. They stay up all night. I never heard of anything like that. I don't know of any pimps I came up with that would stay up all night and miss their rest! That's the name of the pimp game, restin' and dressin' I never heard of niggers staying up all night and supposed to be pimps until now in this era. They sit up in the rain in them cars, all hunched up, til 6 and 7 in the morning. I'd rather work. What gratifications can you get as a pimp if you got to be out there running up and down getting tired. Pimps are not suppose to get tired. Not when I was pimping.

Another point, the best pimps in this country don't have black stables, they pimp on white women.

BLACK COLLEGIAN: A doctor administers medicine, a pharmacist gives out drugs, what does a pimp do?

SLIM: A pimp cons, bamboozles, pressures, schemes and rest and dress. Back in the days when I was a pimp, we individually were our own best company. For instance, I could stay in a motel room for the next five years and never go out, or in any room for that matter. You know why? Because I'm conditioned to be company for my own self. My inner life is very rich. All pimps have to be able to do this because they must play gods to be pimps. When you're pimping you don't confide in anybody. A pimp never does that if he's for real and from the same generation I came from.

But back to the story. So as it turned out finally, Leander collapsed so they literally carried her back into the hotel and put her in the room across the hall. So in about a half hour she was making groaning sounds. Now remember a five dollar bill could have brought a doctor. It wasn't the money. But she was a very beautiful young girl and I had just gotten her and she hadn't proven herself. Pimps must be very careful that they don't show favoritism, especially to a new girl who is beautiful. So I didn't call the doctor. A half hour passed. I put my dog in my arms, Bill Bailey was his name. The door was ajar and here Leander was sitting in a straight back chair completely nude and there was something rather unnatural about her posture. So I said "Leander" and she didn't say anything. She didn't move. I looked over her shoulder and she had her legs spread open and there was a puddle of greenish slime on the chair bottom. What happened was that her appendix had burst and she was dead. That's the one thing that keeps haunting me and that was a crime of omission.

Those on the outside who see pimps don't realize that he's living in a cauldron of hatred that he is responsible for. It's not an easy life. You can't be complacent. Even when you're supposed to be resting your mind has got to be teeming because you are almost literally sitting on... if you've got 5 or 6 women anyone of them might be appearing as a witness in a secret grand jury or something. You just never know and pretty soon all your possessions, the cars and stuff, they're not important. When you were a punk kid you thought it was great. You enjoyed it when you first got it or when you saw somebody else with it, you want it, but when you got it, it's nothing. There's no thrill to any of it because the pressures are so great.

BLACK COLLEGIAN: What attraction does a pimp have for a woman?

SLIM: He's "Svengali" which proves that the pimp is asexual. He's so crazy that he's fascinating. His sex life is that he will lie down full of cocaine and have his girls kissing his feet and licking him and caressing him but he's passive. That's the way we used to pimp. Somebody asked me this, they said "are pimps latent homosexuals?" I said of course they are and some of them are threatened more than others. I've always suspected, even in my own case, that one of the elements of attraction is that a woman in The Life can somehow have her lesbian tendencies gratified, her latent homosexuality gratified by the pimp's latent homosexuality, by the female quotient in her personality. But I can't prove it.

BLACK COLLEGIAN: Do you think that pimping will ever go out of business?

SLIM: No.

BLACK COLLEGIAN: Why not?

SLIM: Because there's a need for it.

BLACK COLLEGIAN: What's the need?

SLIM: There will always be a market for it because there will always be frustrated husbands and there will always be lonely men who can't catch or who don't have the time or who don't want to become involved with a woman. That is what creates the market. It's that there are great numbers of men, black, white, all ethnic groups who figure that it's more economical and less stress involved. Life is so complicated now that women have declared war on men and want even more concessions. Women's lib is going to contribute to an increase in prostitution, because men are becoming, especially young men coming up, they are going to find it increasingly difficult

88

to affect a marriage contract because they are basically cold-blooded young men and they're intelligent and they know the pitfalls. They will be very reluctant to marry because the females that are available to them to marry will have become affected with women's lib in some way. The terms that they'll have to go in on, they just won't submit themselves to that. And then too, their egos are so big. There's just no way. This is why I say that prostitution will increase.

BLACK COLLEGIAN: Any words for college students?

SLIM: Well all I can say is keep your survival kit polished, if you're a nigger. Don't let it rust. Examine it. Open it up and see that it's in good working order with all of its multiplicity of items. Don't let your survival kit get rusty and keep putting new implements in it. Keep enlarging your survival kit. Its principal item surely must be the best possible education that you can get. Keep your mind open. Keep oiling the crevices in the mind so that all of its operable parts will continue to operate at maximal efficiency.

BLACK COLLEGIAN: Thank you.

SLIM: Righteous. Thank you.

1971. Iceberg Slim (foreground) on the streets of Chicago during the filming of the "Iceberg Slim: Up From Under" documentary.

WHAT MAKES A WOMAN GOOD IN BED

Iceberg Slim: ex-pimp

By Wendy Leigh

1977

Iceberg Slim was a pimp for over five hundred women, and is author of the book Pimp *and many others. When I phoned, a deep voice said, "Hello, this is Iceberg, Iceberg Slim." My blood curdled and I nearly cancelled the interview except that I didn't dare. Iceberg greeted me with a handshake outside his house, then took me inside to a decidedly domestic tea with his wife and four children.*

I could never tell if a woman was going to be good in bed until she performed with me. I've known whores who were the ultimate projection of exciting sex, only to discover that they were *not* in bed, because she might end up not making money, which would lead to the worst possible confrontation: between a pimp and a job.

Pimps are asexual. I was in it for the money and not the sex. When you have a stable of twenty girls working for you, you are in trouble if you are into being a superstud. Career pimps, as I was, try to preserve themselves, to conserve their energy. I always appeared very sour, otherwise whores got you in the end. When a pimp was hooked on a whore, we would say, "He has got that bitch's scent up his nose." The essence of the woman got tied up inside their brains, weakening them.

But whores are better in bed than most women. The sexual peak is prior to the menopause for most women, the golden age for a woman to be good in bed. But age is less marketable than youth. Whores are good for acrobatics and slavish devotion - they make the best mechanics. When I say slavish devotion - a whore won't *really* do anything, but she still leaves you with the impression that she has done everything - because whores use their hands, their feet, their voices - they are like quicksilver. They needed to be, because my whores worked eighteen hours a day, and had to bring back $100 a day, even in the thirties.

I like a woman to come to me bringing a reputation for wicked eroticism. Not that she is a pushover, but that she is always free (unlike a whore) to choose whoever she goes to bed with, and that no one forces her or owns her. There is a kind of choreography of sex that matters. Some women, after they have had sex with you for about the third time, have the aptitude to mesh with you. Everything is fluid as you move her through the various sexual positions with the pressure of your fingertips, or even the voice. She flows with you.

Erotic taste buds also make a woman good in bed, when a woman knows what you want without being told, almost by witchcraft. Also, power in bed is very important: a crossbow back, lots of strength, so that you know when you have taken her to the peak, it will be drama the moment you push her off.

I don't think a woman is less good in bed if she takes a long time to come. I am suspicious of a woman whose furnace you can set ablaze immediately, because sometimes she is faking, or is a nymphomaniac and then you can never hope to satisfy her. Some women are very silent in bed, but I think that the best women are always those who carry on an erotic conversation, a reportage of what they are doing while you are in bed. That is important for the man who really considers himself a great lover, because the woman heightens his glorious self-image by reporting along the way. A woman can also create a good self-image for herself by thinking of herself as an assassin, a killer in bed, with the destruction of the man her ultimate goal.

I've never forced a woman to do anything in bed. Women always did what I wanted anyway - they were all good partners and wanted to please me. I am not talking about whores - they try to tire pimps out with fellatio. They do it all the time, even in the car - and they swallow (it kills oral sex if a woman refuses to swallow).

Physical build doesn't make a woman better in bed, just different. Thin women are more susceptible to choreography, more fluidity, but plump women also compete in their own way, with warmth and softness. Chemistry has a lot to do with how good a woman is in bed. It is produced when two psyches meet and their oils, their fluids, coalesce; that is what produces good sex.

ICEBERG SLIM: PIMPING THE PAGE

By Nolan Davis

Players Magazine

Volume 4, No. 1

1977

PLAYERS: You have been described as the best-sellingest black author in America. Why is that?

BECK: Well, if that is true, I would think it's because I've been able to do what any artist must do if he's to rule the greatest possible audience – and that is to bare his emotional structure to the bone. I've noticed the same phenomenon as a speaker. I've been a success as a speaker because I've dared to do that which the audience, collectively, could not do. That is, I have overridden my inhibitions so I can *confess*. It springs from the soul, brother. So many people are dying and crying out to confess. But they lack the courage.

PLAYERS: Do you believe you deserve the success that's come to you?

BECK: Well, I don't know... I know one thing. I'm constantly aware, and appreciative of the fact that I literally have been blessed with the possibility of having two lives within one, getting perhaps the best of both.

PLAYERS: Was the first life an natural premise for the second one?

BECK: Well, our present civilization being what it is, one of the great shocks I got, Nolan, was when I came out of the underworld, I thought that the so-called upper world was entirely different. I mean I didn't realize that they're one and the same. The only thing is that in the upper world, the so-called criminals protect themselves by staying within the law.

PLAYERS: Do you apply what you've learned in the underworld to your operations in the upper world?

BECK: Oh I couldn't have survived if I had not brought that portfolio with me. I was always almost a perfect student of human nature. I had to be to survive in the underworld. And everything that I learned about human nature I apply now. Because a dope peddler, a so-called "ho" – the hustlers I'd grown up with and associated with most of my life – they were human beings, too. So the same rules, the same things I'd learned about them, applied to denizens of the so-called upper world.

PLAYERS: Are you saying that writing is like pimping?

BECK: I'm saying that the transfer from "The Life" to writing served me well in that one has to tell a good story in writing. And the same thing is true, of course, of a pimp.

PLAYERS: Give us an example.

BECK: Well, all right. Hypothetical situation: You have caught a young girl. You want to turn her out. Now. You have to quiz her so that you get an inkling as to what she is so that you will know precisely what emotional buttons to push. Now. The same thing is true with a writer. He has to analyze and evaluate his audience before he writes a word. He has to know what emotional buttons to push. Transfer the technique – or the *awareness*, should I say.

PLAYERS: How does the writer analyze his audience? It's unseen.

BECK: Well, you see first of all, he has a certain publication that he's going to shoot for with his writing. If he's signed by a particular publisher, well then he knows what that publisher's audience is. From precedent. Of course, one doesn't tailor his work precisely. Now one of the difficulties I surmounted with my first book – and I'm proud of that and I always will be proud – is that almost *intuitively* I knew that I had to keep my writing with negligible foggery. I knew that one of the pitfalls was that my ego would go to the page because after all I had a free-floating ego because I was cut loose from the ego-satisfaction of being a pimp, playing God literally. So I did not have that need, that obsession, to indicate to the audience how many long words I knew.

PLAYERS: Are you still playing God?

BECK: Oh no, no, no.

PLAYERS: Doesn't every writer play God?

BECK: Yes. But one can't play God if one is also a father. One of the handicaps, of course, in being a writer is that one has large numbers of children, responsibilities. Ideally a writer should be alone. Most writers – if they're married – inevitably, the wife will soon consider the writing as a rival. And no writer can reach his peak with this kind of *intramural* opposition.

PLAYERS: You're a very eloquent man. Were you always so?

BECK: Not especially eloquent as far as go the standards of the so-called Square World. But I had masterworks of Pimp Strategy and all that stuff, you know, for the jungles of the street. Of course there were some among my associates, man, that I couldn't hold a candle to. Just most of them could outtalk me. But, there was one saving grace. I had a practice. At 2:30 in the morning, they would all stay out until 5 or 6 o'clock in the morning, just hanging out, you know. But I would go in and rest and drink milk and go to sleep. Now. At least dozens of times during those 25 to 30 years, some charming, seemingly wealthy woman who was obviously upper-crust would come into one of these haunts and they'd all take shots at her. But because they were hobbled with the pimp argot, they couldn't pull her. So they would call me and they would say "Slim, come on down here and take a shot." Well, I always read books that I would never even let my friends even know I read. You know, I was a closet pursuer of knowledge. I mean, because look: on several occasions they would see certain things, you know, like Jung and Freud and all and they'd say: "You square-ass motherfucker. There ain't nothing in there motherfucker, that's gonna help you pimp." They would, you know, they would rib me, so I'd hide the fact that I was a seeker of knowledge – above and beyond pimp knowledge, you dig? Even in prison, I wouldn't even go to the yard. I read all the books in four penitentiaries. In the libraries of four penitentiaries, man. And I would have to read from the feeble light off the cell-house walls because they turned the lights off at 9:30, 10 o'clock in those days.

PLAYERS: What were your favorite books?

BECK: Just *all* the classics. And of course psychology, I was just crazy about it. I read the first book that the Menninger Clinic printed, written back in the 30s. Karl Menninger I think it was, *The Human Mind* – whatever the title was. It was elementary, man, but it opened up for me... Man, I thought this was the ultimate in a psychological text. And, man, I just moved up the line like that.

PLAYERS: What was the purpose of reading so many psychology books?

BECK: All right. I had a fancy as far back as 40 years ago when I did my first bit. I've forgotten who the international swindler of women was – Lustig, Count Lustig it was – and I pictured myself being the absolute seducer of high-class rich women. I had a fantasy, man. And I knew that I'd have to rap... *transcendentally*. I knew that even as an embryo would-be swindler and captivator of women, I knew that. But I wasn't cognizant of the fatal handicap that my skin color would offer. Because how many times do you get in position for a shot, even, at the kind of woman that I was prepping for?

PLAYERS: Are you a high-school graduate? College graduate?

BECK: No, not college, no. I was sent to Tuskegee on a scholarship and I then proceeded, of course, so sell whiskey, bootleg, on campus and I was also involved with many of the maidens on the hills around campus. I'd go to the juke joints and I'd seduce them until the bitches would go and, of course, I inherited backlash. One of them pursued me down the main campus street one day with a shard of Coca-Cola bottle and all the students were there, coming in and out, so they sent me home. This, of course, was superimposed on the boot-legging.

PLAYERS: Back to your reading. Has it been helpful to you in your writing today?

BECK: Oh, of course. Without the years and years that I studied psychology on my own, I would not now be able to draw a character. It's extremely expedient. And what helped me even more than that perhaps is the fact that, as a boy, as a pre-teener, and then a few years beyond that, I was fortunate enough to come in contact with lots of white people – even back in those days. As a matter of fact, I played with Italians, I would be a guest at their homes, in and out of their homes, I was exposed to their particular ethnic passion. And then later on, of course, I had a great deal of experience with white women from every social spectrum.

PLAYERS: How does that help your writing?

BECK: Well, it helps me to draw white people realistically.

PLAYERS: Where are you going now with your writing?

BECK: I'm going as far as my capabilities will permit me to. Which is what the artist dreams of.

PLAYERS: Do you have the temperament of an artist?

BECK: I don't know what the temperament of an artist is. But I know what the ideal temperament of an artist should be. And that is, that he must place his work above all else.

PLAYERS: Is that the same as the temperament of a pimp?

BECK: Same thing. So here again we have another transfer. Because a pimp, of course, if he fails as a pimp, then he has the most atrocious affair to deal with. And that is a job.

PLAYERS: Recently, you wrote an article about the loneliness of a super-pimp...

BECK: Ah, the loneliness... yes, the loneliness. Because you see, the only comparison I could make, as a matter of fact, with the loneliness of a writer is the loneliness of a pimp. I'm not talking about a would-be pimp. I'm talking about someone who really understands what pimping is. And by that I mean: no matter what problems I ever had as a pimp, I never got confidential with any woman. I had one woman that I kept for

13 years and I never got confidential with her. Not once was I found in bed *sour*. I always beat her out of the bed, so that when she saw me, I was all fresh, fresh as a rose, while *she* was sour. And I'd be sitting there, like a field marshal, you see, all impeccable. I might even have gone down to the barber shop and gotten myself all refurbished, everything. And there she found me, the gentleman who had gotten slightly sweaty with her during the night perhaps – but I had recouped, you see, and I was still the flawless, infallible Jehovah that I was when we got in bed.

PLAYERS: And the writer?

BECK: Well, of course the writer doesn't even have time to take proper care of himself. He misses meals, he might put in 16 hours a day, he might not take a bath for several days. He becomes haggard when tossed on the horns of a project that he's infatuated with, he's short-tempered, he treats his children as if they were invisible...

PLAYERS: Like a whore...

BECK: Well, in the case of a whore, one has the elegance of the pimp façade and the energy expenditure in the case of the pimp is done in the most sublime setting...

PLAYERS: Is the public not a whore?

BECK: No, no. The public is not a whore.

PLAYERS: Must not the public be seduced?

BECK: No. Because a whore has never been as fickle as the public.

PLAYERS: Ah...

BECK: I mean... I mean how can I say? You have some... some reasonable chart with a whore. But the public – the audience I should say. Whether you're on stage giving a speech or whether you're writing, in all respects the audience is like a whore. They're not interested in what you did yesterday, for instance. *Muthafucker, what did you do today?*

Which could be your current work. Then, of course, they'll heap calumny upon you and reject you and kill you, you see, and then you're dead. So I would say: yes. There is a similarity between an audience and a whore.

PLAYERS: Does the public have to be seduced in similar fashion?

BECK: Ah, seduced to the extent that you reveal your own raw quick to them. You serve as a mirror. Of all the things, through your characters and so forth, you allow people to look there and see themselves without making a commitment.

PLAYERS: Are you a whore?

BECK: I think so. We all are, if you live under capitalism.

PLAYERS: Do you write because you're trying to "expiate," that is "exorcise" the devils of your past?

BECK: I write because of a hoodlum vacuum of ego that I was deprived of when I squared up. That was the source of my suffering. There's no torture worse than that of a pimp who suddenly finds himself bereft of a stable.

PLAYERS: Do you still find the thrill of pimping in your writing?

BECK: I don't think the comparison is exact. But I do get a thrill out of knowing that I've been able to transfer the gifts I had as a pimp to the literary thing. And that is to write stories that large numbers of people remember and are entertained by.

PLAYERS: Usually a writer tries to do more than merely entertain. He tries to inform and persuade.

BECK: Oh yes. I don't try to persuade. I used to be political. When I first started writing. Nothing is worse than to write with a tendency like that. You can't be a true artist. That's what hobbled most of the young black writers that came up in the 60s. They couldn't achieve catharsis. In other words, one must – if he's black or any ethnic – if he's aware of the inequities of this society, *purge* himself, have that catharsis,

101

through his writing, in order to approach the pristine peak that the artist, the true artist, knows.

PLAYERS: You then purge yourself on paper?

BECK: On paper! There's no other way to do it. If you're going to be a writer, see? Because you've got to get it out. You've got to *cleanse* yourself so you can become objective. An artist has to be objective. I can draw a policeman now and get empathy if a policeman occurs in a story of mine. You see, if you never achieve a catharsis, inevitably, you would draw the policeman one-dimensionally as a pure beast. You don't make him human. Because your prejudice has obscured it. And strangulated art.

PLAYERS: Are you still a pimp?

BECK: No, not even in fantasy any more.

PLAYERS: What about in terms of selling your writing?

BECK: Well, if you want to stretch the analogy, I suppose it might.

PLAYERS: Haven't you yourself stretched the analogy? Haven't you used the term "Pimping the Page?"

BECK: But you know why I've never been able to do it? Because of the torturous labor that writing is.

PLAYERS: Mmmmm hummm.

BECK: If it weren't so goddam hard man, I could make the analogy. But it's so hard...

PLAYERS: Mmmmm hummm.

BECK: I mean to produce a quality piece, it's *haaaaard!*

PLAYERS: Are you a masochist?

BECK: I think all writers have to be. I'm talking about serious writers – like yourself. You know you *love* it. You love that pain, that lonely pain.

PLAYERS: Is there any sadism connected to this?

BECK: Yeah. We inflict that, we often inflict that upon the audience. You know, two sides of a coin. But invariably, we inflict it upon the people around us, like our wives and our children, when we suffer, you know.

PLAYERS: Would you say you've achieved a balance or homeostasis between your inner sections and the outer realities?

BECK: Yes. And I've achieved it through what I call "The Overview." The way I interpret "overview" personally is that I will not permit any traumatic event, person or force to deal my writing and my life a fatal blow. I will not gnaw on personal tragedy like some psychotic canine. When the deed has been done to me, whether advertently or inadvertently, I will simply forget that, I don't conduct vendettas against people, objects or circumstances.

PLAYERS: You're telling what you *don't* do. But what *are* you doing?

BECK: Staying above it with The Overview.

PLAYERS: What does that lead you to? What is your object? What do you want?

BECK: To avoid trauma. So that the work is the most therapeutic, that transcends everything!

PLAYERS: Do you think you'd have problems if you didn't write?

BECK: Oh, would I? I'd probably relapse into some criminal pursuit. Connected with pimping.

PLAYERS: Writing, then, for you is a savior?

BECK: And the purest escape.

PLAYERS: *Purifying?*

BECK: Yes, it's purifying because it keeps you on the forthright. Let's face it: when you've been a pimp for as long as I have, it's in every pore, in every atom of your being. And it is only through illusion that you convince yourself that it's dead. Hail, hail! The monster's dead. You know in your secret heart that the monster might very well be activated by external forces. And then I was a junkie, you see. And afflicted with the permanent imprint of the junkie and all of the spin-out, phantasmagoria, the lusting, even when one had kicked one's habit. There's a *lusting*, lusting for that feeling, that sensation, because there is no sensation – even the hell of the writer when he's in the throes of creation, as magnificent as that is – that can compare with the chemical rush of a speed-ball. But one is therapeutic and the other is hemlock.

PLAYERS: You have to avoid hemlock.

BECK: Oh ho like the plague! I don't feel that I will relapse. But it's better that they not recreate in me the ingrams of phantasmagoria.

PLAYERS: How do you go about staying away from it?

BECK: It's easy. I've withdrawn completely. I seldom come out.

PLAYERS: Of the house, you mean.

BECK: Of course. I stay in and work. Just work.

PLAYERS: Well what do you do when you stay in and work?

BECK: Just work.

PLAYERS: Type, you mean.

BECK: No, I'm writing. I write long-hand and I have my work typed up. And when I'm not in the physical process of working, that is with pen in hand on paper, then I'm seeming

104

to be day-dreaming. But I'm not. I'm reading on the ceiling characters for yet another story. And I hallucinate their voices and try to get the texture of their voices so I can become acquainted with them. That's why I can write so fast. When I get ready to go to the page, I've already had this prior association with them. And great snatches of dialogue have been written on the ceiling already.

PLAYERS: You once were a creature of the night. Do you write at night?

BECK: Ideally, from 2am to 7 in the morning.

PLAYERS: What do you do after that?

BECK: I write on the ceiling until I go to sleep. Again.

PLAYERS: Do you make a lot of money from your books?

BECK: No. When you say "a lot of money," you know to a pauper a hundred-dollar bill is a fortune. And then a John Paul Getty, a hundred-thousand is a pittance. But I'm not a seeker of fortune. All that I aspire to is to have comforts, and to be cushioned so I can have the most magnificent luxury there is. And that is one of privacy, so that I might write.

PLAYERS: Do you find that you have become quite a different person from the person who wrote *Pimp?*

BECK: Oh, have I!

PLAYERS: Do you find it hard to stay in touch?

BECK: No, I don't have any problems.

PLAYERS: Do you find it hard to be black?

BECK: Yeah. Not any more, because of The Overview.

PLAYERS: Is your wife white?

BECK: Cajun. Cajun, Indian and French. Which makes for some rather good cooking, and devotion and love, as you well know.

PLAYERS: When do you think you will die?

BECK: I don't there's any of us will ever die. When you say "die," you mean conventionally? You mean physically? I don't know, I don't spend my time with... Here again, in Overview, you know that everything is an illusion anyway. Life itself.

PLAYERS: Life is an illusion.

BECK: Yeah. Sex is an illusion, everything is an illusion.

PLAYERS: And are you about giving illusions?

BECK: Right. And baring the raw quick.

PLAYERS: Are you satisfied with your progress as a writer so far?

BECK: No, because I started late. And given the Biblical actuarial estimate, it seems to me that I've only got maybe 10 years. And writing being the inconjurable that it is, I wish that I'd started at your age or even younger, so I would at least have some remote chance of becoming the absolute artist. Because every day, every day, is a reminder of how little I know as a writer.

PLAYERS: Do you believe in reincarnation?

BECK: No, not as such. But I can't believe that there is just oblivion, black oblivion.

PLAYERS: What do you believe, then?

BECK: Well, I just believe that the spirit will survive.

PLAYERS: Why do you avoid discussing in any detail anything other than writing? Or pimping?

BECK: Well, it might be because of the fact that I have had to use my energies both in the pimp life and as a writer to attempt to fit some kind of harness on my skills.

PLAYERS: Have you ever been a homosexual?

BECK: No.

PLAYERS: How did you satisfy yourself then, during all that time in prison?

BECK: I learned to make consummate love to myself.

PLAYERS: Masturbation?

BECK: Exactly.

PLAYERS: Why do they call you "Iceberg?"

BECK: Actually I don't deserve that moniker because at the time that I got it, I was frosted and refrigerated with a skull full of cocaine and I reacted to a traumatic situation in an icy manner, which prompted a pimp friend of mine to rah-rah at me for having been so cool under fire. But it was artificially induced, you see. My cool.

PLAYERS: What was the situation?

BECK: We were in a bar. There were two dudes squabbling behind us. One of them drew a gun and shot, grazed his adversary, and the bullet that grazed this gentleman went through my hat at the crown and knocked it onto the bar top. Of course, I was at the moment contemplating the millions of bubbles in a glass of 7-Up, trying to count them before they would pop and evaporate. I wasn't really there at all. Of course I reacted, you know, in a way that one would when they've snorted up a solid roll of pure crispy-thrust.

PLAYERS: Do you plan to write about anything other than pimps and con men?

BECK: Oh, of course, of course. As a matter of fact, I told you one of the reasons that I'm very proud of my chances as a writer is that I can draw white people quite well, especially white women. And I plan to do a novel with a white woman focal. There'll be black people in the story. In fact, there'll be at least one black man who'll share billing. A poignant affair of the heart.

PLAYERS: Did you ever think about writing a book of philosophy?

BECK: No, because I haven't done the prerequisite reading that one must do so that one will have shape and form for that kind of writing. I've been forced to write commercial stuff. That luxury has been denied me. To even think about it... Of course I've gone to the essay form. I did that in *The Naked Soul*. But I had the awesome figure of James Baldwin, as does any writer who approaches the essay form – I have James Baldwin hovering over my shoulder. But I was surprised that I came off rather well.

PLAYERS: You're wearing a Superfly-like hairdo and snazzy vestments. Why?

BECK: It's all in keeping, I suppose, with the old conditioning. I suppose it's the last residue of a pimp syndrome. And perfectly harmless, of course.

PLAYERS: Of course. Have you been pimping in this interview?

BECK: No, man. Why should I? I've just tried to bear the raw quick as usual, give you a glimpse of my naked soul...

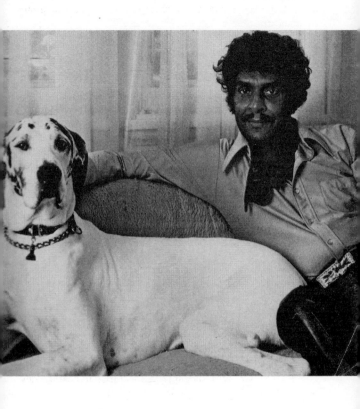

Circa 1977.

Courtesy PLAYERS Magazine, USA.

AFRICAN AMERICAN AUTHOR, LECTURER, DIES AT 74 IN LOS ANGELES

Press Release

Holloway House Publishing Co.

1992

Robert Beck, one of America's best selling African American authors, who introduced a generation of Americans to the little known dark side of ghetto street life in Chicago, died Thursday, April 30, 1992 in Los Angeles at age 74. He is survived by his wife, Diane Millman Beck and daughter, Melodie.

He has written seven books about his life as a hustler and a one time pimp, using his street player's handle, "Iceberg Slim." His first book, *Pimp: the Story of My Life*, explores what drove him to brutalize and dehumanize women and himself while pimping in Chicago from the late 1930's to about 1961. Over the eight years following the publication of *Pimp*, Beck wrote and Holloway House published six additional books, all drawn from personal experiences and from street people he knew. They were *Trick Baby*, made into a major motion picture released by Universal, *Mama Black Widow*, *The Naked Soul of Iceberg Slim*, *Long White Con*, *Death Wish* and *Airtight Willie and Me*. All are in print. His publisher, Holloway House, Los Angeles, California, has just introduced all his titles in a commemorative silver edition celebrating the 25th anniversary since publication of his first book.

Robert Beck was born August 4, 1918 in Chicago and lived much of his childhood in Milwaukee and Rockford, Illinois before returning to Chicago as a teenager. His father deserted the family when Robert was a child. He attended Tuskagee Institute briefly in the mid 1930's at the same time as Ralph Ellison was there (they did not know each other.) He stopped writing in 1977, telling a reporter, "I have nothing left to say." He spent the latter years of his life lecturing at high schools and colleges about the degradation of street life: hustling, drug dealing and pimping. His books have sold in excess of six million copies and are included as recommended reading in most Black studies programs. Now he is an inspiration for many of the rap singers. Ice-T said in a recent Newsweek Magazine article that he took his name from Iceberg Slim. Beck's books have become urban classics among young black males who live daily in the words in which Robert Beck has spawned.

ROBERT " *Iceberg Slim* " BECK

August 4, 1918 - April 30, 1992

Holloway House Publishing Co.

FOND MEMORIES OF A DIFFERENT MAN

By Jim Cleaver

Los Angeles Sentinel

9th July 1992

The young folk won't remember him. The old folk who do remember him will recall with some sense of distain. In their minds, he was, at best, a disreputable character. I first met Robert Beck at the Old Southwest Camera Store over on Vermont Avenue about 24 years ago.

One of the clerks in the store had told him I was a regular customer and one Saturday morning he waited until I came in. He introduced himself to me and explained he had wanted to meet me. He told me he has written several books and was working on another at the time.

This man, this Robert Beck, went on to explain he had even sold one or two of his books to the movies, but there seemed to be some problem getting the scripts produced.

I had read his first and probably most famous book, and I had wondered about the idea that someone from the streets, who was still making his living from the streets, would "tip his mitt": that is, give up his trade secrets and still be respected in the streets.

To the uninitiated, Bob Beck had another name. He was the infamous Iceberg Slim, who's "Autobiography of a Pimp" became one of the most widely read and well-hidden books of all time.

We had one whale of a conversation. It started at the counter in the Southwest Camera Store and moved to the curb in front of the store, where we sat and talked for what must have been hours.

He told me he had "squared" up and married a "square" girl and she was pregnant even as we spoke. He talked about the life he had lived and the effect the life had had on him and how, one day, after his mother died, he decided to give up the street life and become just like everybody else.

Bob Beck liked old cars and he owned a Lincoln Continental II. He had restored it and it looked totally out of place on Vermont in front of a vacant theatre that Saturday morning.

That was the first of many conversations we were to have. Most of them were on the phone, but occasionally we would meet at the old Operation Breadbasket meetings on Saturday mornings and Beck would give an impromptu performance or reading of some of his work. The crowds would go wild, and when the meetings were over, he would literally be mobbed by the people who had been in the audience.

This was a gentle Robert Beck, a man who held people spellbound as he told his stories.

High school kids would cover "Autobiography of a Pimp" with plain brown paper and carry it along with their other school books. Matronly housewives would hide the book between the mattress and the boxspring, so their children or their spouses wouldn't see them reading this "piece of trash."

Bob Beck died several weeks ago here in Los Angeles. There was not a lot of fanfare at his funeral. That seems sad, because Beck tried to make amends for whatever wrongs he committed against society.

He went to jail, served his time and then came out and tried to educate young black men against his former lifestyle. He showed them the fallacy of that life and preached to them they should get educations and try to make it in the legitimate world.

Maybe some listened and heard his pleas. Hopefully, there are some young men and women who learned from the mistakes of Iceberg Slim.

This corner will remember Robert Beck, a man who turned the corner and tried to show others the same path. He was 74 years old when he died at the end of April and the last 25 years of his life were spent trying to do good.

He will be fondly remembered for that effort.

SEARING PROSE OF THE UNDERWORLD ICEBERG:
OBITUARY OF ROBERT BECK

By Cathal Tohill

The Guardian

8th August 1992

ROBERT Beck, who has died aged 73, was an anti-hero in the true sense of the word. Unconventional yet compelling, he gave a tragic majesty to the world of the ultimate outsider - the pimp.

Born in Chicago, he adopted the street name Iceberg Slim at the age of 19 and became one of those high-earning folk heroes, an urban pimp. After 25 years in the 'fast track' he'd had enough . . . he left behind his life as a pimp and petty criminal and carved out a career as one of America's best-selling black authors. His first book, Pimp: the Story of My Life (1969) has sold over two million copies and is still a solid seller.

Pimp paved the way for the spate of 'streetwise' fiction that would follow, and from Yardie to Donald Goines they all owe a debt to Iceberg Slim. His books are more than just the roadmaps that all the young contenders try to follow, they have the all-important stamp of authenticity drawing their audience to them like a magnet, but alienating writers and other cultural critics with one fell swoop.

With searing honesty, street cool and crusading passion, Pimp delineates all the factors that pushed, pulled and propelled its author into the dog-eat-dog underworld of the pimp game. It's a remarkable feat handled with vitality and detachment, in short the very qualities that took him to the top of his nefarious trade. If the subject matter had been different he might have been hailed as a major new black writing talent. Like all his books, Pimp documents the highs and lows of the hustling world with unmerciful candour. It's a roller-coaster ride whose destination is oblivion, emotional isolation and lonely self-awareness. This gnawing truth is overlooked by those who dismiss him.

As a youngster he was a 'sweet boy' with 'legitimate charm', but he found these qualities useless if he was to make the grade as a hustler. To succeed in the pimp world you had to have 'implacability' and 'control' over your emotions. He kept a 'steel lid' on himself, and when he became a full-time pimp, he chillingly admitted, 'he didn't smile for decades'. This kind of aloofness and self-control paid dividends.

It drew the right type of women and made them easier to handle. His ice-cool front gave him the distance necessary for his Machiavellian manipulations, it also made it easier for him to project emotional force with complete intensity. In the long run there was a price to pay.

His schooling as a hustler totally changed his life, leaving him permanently branded as an outsider. He tried normality and the 'straight life' but never quite managed to settle into it unobtrusively. He was always slightly out-of-synch. As a father he couldn't smile or play normally with his kids, and his past tainted more than just his private life - it also added to his cultural isolation. Inside the black community his reputation was mixed. To the kids on the street he was a 'folk hero'. To the spokesmen he was an embarrassment, a facet of urban life they'd hoped would disappear. Each successive book added to his status as one of the best-selling black authors in the US. After the success of The Godfather, Universal Pictures bought up the film rights to Pimp but the project was considered 'too hot' and put on hold. His novel, Trick Baby: The Story of a White Negro, was filmed in 1973 and drew good reviews. Despite his talent he was left floating around the margin. For anyone else the situation would look like gloom and doom. Yet he managed to turn it on its head and transcend it.

Each successive book seemed bleaker and more brutal than the last, almost as if it reflected his heroic isolation. On the one hand he was a 'local hero' and 'ghetto voice'. On the other he shunned street contact, and was ignored by the media.

Sometimes he welcomed his outsider status, and embraced it as an inevitable part of his nature. He chuckled wryly as he declared 'I am a loner to the extent that I put my own shadow outside the door and lock it out'. Towards the end he put it 'to be a loner is perfect. To be gregarious and on the edge, is horrible. But when you're a loner there's a kind of perverse joy, inner joy.' Robert Beck ('Iceberg Slim'), August 4, 1918 died April 28, 1992.

THE HOUSE THAT BLACKS BUILT

By Peter Gilstrap

Los Angeles New Times

Vol 3 Number 42

15th October 1998

In 1969 Holloway House released *Pimp*, edited by Milton Van Sickle, a former metallurgist, Great Lakes oar boat deckhand, and electroplater who was with Holloway from '65 to '69.

"I read *Pimp* and told my bosses it was the best book we ever published." Says the retired editor.

Pimp was the first of seven books that would chronicle Slim's life in a world decent folk may loath to tread but *love* to read about.

According to Holloway, Slim alone has sold more than six million books – making him one of the biggest-selling black American authors in history – and his legendary first work, *Pimp: the Story of My Life*, has been translated into French, Spanish, Italian, Dutch, Swedish and Greek.

"Bob was an incredible human being," says Bentley Morriss [of Holloway.] "I think he had an IQ of 165. He was charismatic, articulate, charming, vain, an imposing figure and dressed immaculatley. Had he not moved in that particular genre, he could have been anything he wanted. An outstanding politician, a major civic servant, just anything he wanted. He had enormous stature, didn't use expletives, had incredible depth, and yet there was nothing ostentatious about the guy."

When he was coming up on Chicago's west side, Odie Hawkins knew Iceberg Slim as a neighbourhood character.

"I lived at 38th and Lake Park when I was 12, 14. It was a red-light district, and Slim was just simply one of several pimps." Hawkins says. "I lived in a building called the Alamo Hotel. Picture the hotels on Figueroa Street, four flights, and we lived on the thrird floor. The first and second floor were transient, it was where the girls turned tricks and Iceberg Slim was one of the people who came in. At that point, he wasn't a major league pimp – he didn't have nine girls, he had maybe three or four."

"He was a great, great talker, a very intelligent man," recalls Hawkins. "He and another pimp named Big Al used to have philosophical talks sitting on the front steps of the building. I was 12, 14, and I looked at him in the same way that a lot of the major-league crack dealers right now are big to the kids. They got big cars, they wear a lot of gold, and they seem to be able to do what they want to do. Iceberg Slim had a certain kind of status because he was a very sharp dresser, he drove a big car, and he seemed to be someone you should look up to. When he came out to LA, to the *in* community the guy was sort of a surprise because *Pimp* wasn't the best written book in the world, but he was telling something about a world that most people have no knowledge of at all."

According to Morriss, *Pimp* "didn't catch on right off the bat. We tried to advertise in the *New York Times* and they wouldn't accept it because of the title. We raised havoc, but we didn't get anywhere. Here we were, a small niche publisher stuck on the West Coast in the colonies of the United States – and the venerable *New York Times*, no way were they going to kowtow to us."

Slim made an appearance on a popular local talk show hosted by the late Joe Pyne; that did the trick.

"He just created a revolution locally," says Morriss. "Every bookstore in the city was calling us." That and a lot of word of mouth provided the catalyst for the ascension of *Pimp*. God knows the reviews, rave or otherwise, weren't flowing in.

"Paperbacks essentially do not garner any review acceptability," explains Morriss. "But we did get a lot of press in the black community, and we did get stories in *The Washington Post* and the *Detroit Free Press*, but not book reviews. They did it because it was a sensational story talking about a subculture."

With the book catching on, Slim spoke about his life and wicked ways and lessons learned on the college circuit where Morriss says the author "was mobbed" at each appearance. Slim used to tell them, "There are three ways to get out of the ghetto. 1) dead in a basket, 2) in handcuffs, 3) with a college degree." Morriss says.

Beyond the period hip cache that Slim embodied, his crushed velvet voice and mellifluous phrasing were hypnotic tools. In the mid-'70s the author released *Reflections*, an album of spoken word basted over a lazy last call jazz background. (It was reissued on the Infinite Zero label in 1994.)

Though he thought of his pimping years and later literary success as a stab at white oppression, and greatley admired Huey Newton and the Black Panthers (this was the period when *Pimp* was on the shelves with *The Autobiography of Malcolm X* and Eldridge Cleaver's *Soul On Ice*) the extremist Panther crowd saw him as a black man exploiting his race for the white dollar.

But if *Pimp* makes it to movie theatres, a new generation of potential Slim fans will be turned onto the master, generating plenty of white and black dollars.

Over the years Hollywood has come calling at Holloway: in 1973 Slim's *Trick Baby* was made into a film starring Kiel Martin and Ted Lange, who would go on to tend bar aboard the *Love Boat*. Currently two of Donald Goines' books are under option, as is Slim's *Mama Black Widow*. *Pimp* seems the most likley candidate coming to a theater near you: Fine Line Pictures has comissioned a screenplay with Quincy Jones attached as producer and Ice Cube is set to play the man from whom he took the first half of his name.

But whether or not any of these films will end up on the big screen is anybody's guess. It would be a nice boost for sales, of course, but Holloway has always ridden along on its own unique inertia, supplying what its readers want.

"To me, he's probably one of the best American authors there ever was," says Bruce Rubenstein, who co-wrote the screenplay with Rob Weiss. "I just think the guy is just such an incredible, original writer: he's like Bukowski. When I read *Pimp*, I was just so enthralled by the book, I just couldn't put it down. It's brutal, brutal stuff, but it's got poetry, you know?"

According to Rubenstein, the film won't be updated with current street phrases, nor will it fall into the tired Blaxploitation slot.

"I think that's why so many studios were afraid of it," he says. "The language is so hard, the messages are hard, they're real. We tried to stay really close to the book, we really tried to capture Iceberg Slim's voice. What seperates it from Blaxploitation is that Robert Beck was a brilliant guy, a profound guy, and he kind of reinvented the language. We were really trying to transcend the hip-hop thing, because a lot

121

of the guys who were interested in doing the project initially wanted to change all the dialogue to hip-hop, and we were pretty dead against that. It's a biopic, it's a really dark, interesting look at The Life."

Circa 1977.

An Interview with Misty Beck

By Ian Whitaker

Los Angeles

15th April 2009

IAN: Did your father advise you on how to interpret his book *Pimp*?

MISTY: I'll be honest with you; my dad did not speak about his writing with me. That and *The Naked Soul* are, to me, the most real of his stories. His other stories are more character built-on situations over the years. Whereas those [in *Pimp*] really are something he's writing very personally about. That was his first book and I think that he put a lot into it; a lot of himself obviously.

I don't think there are too many things that aren't true in there. I believe that he had definitely poured himself and really opened up with that book: therapy to get something out.

It's a twisted tale, a lot of it. Some of the things he did as a young man... But, for what it's worth, he was definitely someone who'd seen things. Back in those days as a black man, pimping was the game so to speak; he did it really well, lived his life!

IAN: How real was the character Iceberg Slim?

MISTY: I don't know if this is a secret; I think that it's a secret; I think that it's something that my mom actually says [in her documentary interview] because I was in the room. I did her makeup for it. I remember her at some point saying - and I think that they are going to use it - she said that that character in *Pimp*, his persona, it was made up.

I have to be honest with you: I think that everyone embellishes in storytelling, if you're a good writer. And he was a good writer. There's embellishing on his characters and who he was. He was rolling as a pimp in Chicago, in the streets, the jungle, that definitely happened, but my mom said that the name Iceberg Slim was not his street name when he was a pimp. I don't think anyone knows that, people think that he used to go by that name on the street. That was the character name for the novel actually.

IAN: Do you know what his name was?

MISTY: I don't even know if he had one of those. If you think back of *Superfly* and movies such as those, these coined phrase names came out of daddy and Donald Goines, if you will. They really did.

IAN: Ironically, your father's message in *Pimp* was not to be a pimp...

MISTY: He did speak of it as a disease that he had, that he overcame and I think that he did have a lot of pride in doing that. But ironically, a lot of people, they don't see that part of the message.

IAN: They don't get past the infatuation?

MISTY: They don't get past the glamour and the pimp of it all and the coolness of the whole game. You don't really have to read between the lines that he was a reformed street-monster and basically... there's a lot of pimps in the world Ian, you usually don't know about them because they usually die in the streets, they don't usually make it out and they defiantly don't write seven novels.

I think he turned the bad of what he did into something positive by regurgitating it out on these books, because I do think it did some therapy for him for what he did.

And he enjoyed steering people away from that life. It may not seem that way, because for who reads a bible it's all perception, so if you pick up his book you might perceive something else. But I can definitely say that he would want people to learn from his books and not go down that path.

IAN: He was a successful criminal, and then he was a successful writer...

MISTY: If he could have applied himself to other things: had he been dealt different cards, maybe a different skin, in those days... Again, growing up in Chicago, in that era, black people weren't allowed to..., you know history.

IAN: Besides the guilt debt he felt regarding his mother, do you know if he felt guilty about his past, a debt to society?

MISTY: I would have to say he didn't regret too much except for his mother's passing.

I think that it would be silly for someone as strong-minded as him to even regret that lifestyle, because that's what made him and that's what made him able to tell his story to people. It was something that had to happen, that he went through that. I don't think that he regretted it.

I guess there would be some regret, but he didn't express it. I guess there would be some regret if there were certain women you treated very badly. But I would say that his mother was his biggest loss, or regret, in his life.

IAN: In the song *Mama Debt* he tells his mother that he's retired, but she tells him not to con her.

MISTY: Yeah, that is true. Something he said he did think about often: a *lot* of regret with the mother thing.

A lot of street pimps... they have a hatred for their mother that comes from whatever... I don't know if they see a lot of men in and out of their house. There are certain things that drive that hate. I guess they have a hatred of themselves and then in the reflection it would be the mother. He probably never did deal with it.

IAN: Was your dad religious?

MISTY: No. We grew up in a crazy environment. There's no religion...

IAN: But his mother was deeply religious...

MISTY: He kind of felt it was a barrier in-between him and his mom. It would stop him from getting inside of her head even. It was a turnoff to him.

IAN: What did he believe in?

MISTY: He believed in evolution. He also believed it was lights out when you die.

He's like, "I'm not gonna see my mom again. That's just a fantasy, the whole JC thing where people pray to a god." He would say things like, "If there really was - and I ain't saying there was a JC - he was dirty; he was blacker than night; his feet looked like Hell; his hair was disheveled." [Laughter] Definitely not a pretty man with long blonde hair, in a white dress, with blue eyes.

Fatherhood

IAN: Has the fact that your father was once a pimp affected your life?

MISTY: Being teenage girls, especially, it was rather embarrassing if someone asked what your dad did. I always said he was a writer, but then of course, what's the next question? "What does he write?"

You know, *now*, these are easy things you can say and explain to people: he was a pimp, but when he was a father he was a writer.

IAN: In *The Naked Soul*, your father states that one of the most important questions he's been asked is if his former life will affect his children. His response is that he has confidence in you and that you'll be clever enough to deal with it.

MISTY: Which is interesting, because it's not like we had any tools to deal with that. I'd say he was a writer and say I don't know what he writes.

At one point James, my son's father, was in and out of county jails and he did go to prison and he told me once on a phone call, "Wow! You know what? Your dad is really, really famous in here!" and that didn't make me feel good, I was like eighteen or something. I was like "Oh that's a *great* place to be famous, a bunch of junkies, pushers, pimps and hookers." My dad was actually still alive at the time.

IAN: How was it for Iceberg Slim to have three daughters?

MISTY: I have this picture with him and this big white dog in it. He was, I think, on his third novel. He just has the coldest look on his face. And he really *wasn't!* [Laughs]

I mean we really changed his life! He said it was like a curse, you know, to have three daughters. Because I mean, come on, look what he used to do! Then he would have the rest of his life to ponder and worry about what man is going to be coming through and treating us like hoes.

My sisters are beautiful, and to him that was a horrible thing. He wished that we were all three hundred pounds and horrible grotesque pigs with warts on our faces or something! [Laughter] I was young and awkward. He never really saw me grow up…

They were already extremely pretty back then in the 80s and that bothered him. He had pictures of us all over his room. But he wasn't appreciative… that we were [attractive]. My sister Camille was living kind of a wild Hollywood lifestyle. It was hard on him. Let's just put it that way.

IAN: Did he give you advice on your relationships?

MISTY: Yeah, no relationships! I never talked about dating anyone with my father. He would probably prefer us to be nuns wearing chastity belts.

He definitely talked about men and said that they're pretty much out to do one thing to you: if it's not to get you pregnant, it's to turn you out somehow! He wanted to scare that into us and steer us away from it.

IAN: How would he try to influence you?

MISTY: He was a wonderful talker. I mean he told stories to you just like he would be writing them. Like he could make up a whole scenario of what James was gonna do to me and it would be an *interesting story* – although it would be about me!

He was great storyteller. He was often on the phone with Mike Tyson during his heydays and Mike Tyson just loved, I think, listening to the stories. He had a very domineering, deep voice of command. He had a lot of command in his voice. He commanded a lot of your attention when he spoke.

I mean, honestly, he's a storyteller: I think every conversation that you would have with him would turn into some type of story. And then he would add you in somehow! You know... if he's giving you advice he really wouldn't say, "Now here's what I'm gonna tell you to do." He would say, "I'll tell you about a *girl* who would behave like *you*..." and then he would make up the character! And it's kind of shitty [laughs] especially if it's about your boyfriend that you're crazy in love with. And the outcome of the story was like usually really bad!

IAN: Were his predictions accurate?

MISTY: My dad was kind of a fortune teller... he could kind of perceive. I wish I would have paid more attention, I was so young... I could have used and applied so much more of whatever he was trying to teach me. It's unfortunate.

I appreciate it now and honestly, he had my son's father down - except for the beating me up part - he never laid a hand on me. He was a, "Cheating, lying son-of-a-bitch!" He turned out to be that!

He said when I have the baby, he said, "That's when the cheating will start. That son-of-a-bitch will never take care of the baby; you'll be stuck with him, living with your mother." and you know what? That's exactly what happened! [Laughs] I lived at my mom's house for a good nine years after we split up.

My father also said that because of the prison thing and his street life, that [James] would possibly give me - if not AIDS, which was just coming around – he said that I'd wind up with some kind of STD that would blind me. Well, it was the girl in the stories he told me.

He really did get everything right except for two really bad things, a STD and violence. I guess they could have happened if I had stayed longer. I definitely got out in time.

IAN: He didn't meet your boyfriend?

MISTY: Absolutely not. I had a strange relationship with [my dad] because I got married when I was eighteen and had a son when I was twenty and he was not happy with my choice of husband, because he was a convict! [Laughter]

Another of the reasons is that when I was pregnant with my son... I was nineteen, I'd finished high school - it wasn't like I was some teenage dropout - and I was married, it's not like I was out of wedlock.

I got married too young in his eyes and I realized [my husband] was not on the best track back then, but my dad didn't want anything to do with my son and he was very abusive while I was pregnant. If I called him he would say that I'm going to start popping kids out left and right; I'm never gonna have a life; this guy's gonna wind up beating me up then he's gonna leave me. And he was right about most of the stuff except the beating up. But he was a cheater and a liar. It was a young love that he didn't accept and you know how young girls are: they fall in love.

At one point [my dad] did want to finally make amends with me, but I was so pissy and angry and holding grudges, which unfortunately has been a big part of my family. A lot of us hold grudges in our family and I try not to be like that, but I held a very tight grudge on my son thing, because he was upsetting me during my pregnancy. "*I'm* not gonna be a part of that kid's life, I tell you that much." So I'd say, "You're right, you'll never see him."

I kind of had what he had, his mamma debt: I have a daddy debt, that's me. There's so much that obviously, being grown now years later; lived a fuller life; I'd have never treated my dad that way. I'd have tried to get through to him.

My dad was upset with me and we never really got it back together before his death. I was twenty-two when he passed away in 1992. I just couldn't get to him because there was a riot going on in Los Angeles. It was on the day of those Rodney King riots and he was in a hospital in South Central. I don't know if you saw on the news, but we were pretty locked down during those riots.

Unfortunately, he did pass away. I don't think he actually knew he was dying. I think that he wanted to see my... he hadn't seen my son: that was a big deal. So I have some regrets there, I'm saddened by that.

IAN: What was the reason he was in hospital?

MISTY: He had gangrene. He actually entered the hospital for an infection and they wanted to remove his leg from the knee down to stop it spreading, because gangrene will kill you if it gets in your blood stream.

Melody told me that they were trying with antibiotics to stop it, but he was going to loose half of his leg and really didn't want to not have his limb. He was really, really upset, he kind of willed himself to death. He died in his sleep as far as we know.

Melody thinks he was strong enough to even will himself to death. I mean he worried so much. Although he didn't dress up any more he really did care about his looks and that is kind of a pimp trait isn't it? And he didn't want to be this old, you know, ugly, legless guy, he was telling her.

IAN: Your sister's names Camille and Melody feature in Iceberg's books. Did your father tell you how he chose your name?

MISTY: My middle name on my birth certificate is Misty. My mom named me Misty. My dad named me Bellissa and my brother is Robin Bell Beck and do you know that name? Isn't that a familiar name to you, Bell? Baby Bell, that's like a pimp, right, so I didn't like my name. But he the always called me it. He called me Bell for short and it aggravated me because I was closer to my mother.

I was five when they split. So there was this mother turning a teenage daughter against her father - they do it all the time - my mom did tell me that he suggested an abortion. They were very hard to get in the 1970s: I was born in 1970. You know, they were doing them with coat hangers in alleys. It wasn't really done all the time. He didn't want me. Unfortunately my dad didn't want her to get pregnant again. He definitely didn't want another daughter.

IAN: How did the things that your mother told you about him affect your relationship with him?

MISTY: When I was a crazy teenager arguing with him I would say, "You named me that shitty name because of a pimp! My mom told me! And that's why you named Robin that, because we're not really like your kids. But you love Melody and Camille." because he named Camille Mary after his mother. His mother's name was Mary and Camille's middle name is Mary. That was a loving gesture, to name her after his dear mother who he loved and didn't have chance to make things right with.

So I was like, "Where the hell did you get Bellissa from? It bothers me."

IAN: What was his reply to you?

MISTY: He said that he liked the name. He said it's a beautiful name. He said that he really didn't name me after the pimp. But he named my brother Bell and there's just some weird connection that used to bother me. It was a crowbar between us because I felt disrespected with my name for some reason. I think my mom planted those seeds by the way.

My name was Bell until as soon as they split up, then my mom never called me that again. I was so young that my middle name became my first name throughout school.

IAN: Did he say where the name Camille was from?

MISTY: He said that he liked the name. And he named my sister Melody also.

IAN: You've told me that your dad was quite a strict person with you.

MISTY: I thought he was the meanest, strictest person. And I didn't even have to check-in to him, remember. I didn't live with him. I used to just skip school and visit with him, so just those couple of hours when we were cutting our classes. It was just like the military sometimes.

My sisters eased my mind later on, after his death, but I always thought that I got the military treatment more so because, 1) I was closer to my mom; and 2) when I was five my mom changed my name, I never went by that name, [Bellissa] which he thought was a slap in the face, and I thought it was a slap in the face that he named me it.

To me it seemed so military to me, like, "Stay in line!" Not as fun to talk to as my sister's recollection of being around him... a lot more lighthearted and interesting and fun. I felt kind of like he's an asshole! [Laughter]

IAN: When you say military, how do you mean?

MISTY: Just like if you were in the service, you know, "Walk straight!" The way people would talk down to a solider when you're in a training camp; it was more like a training camp than fatherly advice. In my face like "Straighten your ass up... or this is what's gonna happen."

Over the years it was apparent that he had separate relationships, very similar with those two, but with me... He had separate rules for each of us, I guess. To me I thought his rules were a little heavy. *They weren't!* Now that I'm thirty-eight years old Ian, I mean give me a break... I was a teenage girl smoking weed, stealing his pot, skipping school, dating a convict. I would be kind of military on my daughter too if I knew what he knew, right? [Laughter]

IAN: How would you see your dad when you were a child and you were living with your mom?

MISTY: Because at one point I used to skip school when I was in high school, everyone does that. I had this friend Tiffany, this white girl who was kind of crazy and she liked to smoke pot. So did I back then.

So we would take this free bus ride down from Hollywood to my dad's house on Crenshaw and I would just kind of pop up, so then he would buy us Church's chicken, it was a chicken place across. He'd give me some money, like five bucks, so we'd go down there.

He still smoked pot. To cut a long story short, we would steal my dad's weed if he went to the bathroom! I took some of his stash, it was on his nightstand.

IAN: Was he well-known in the neighborhood?

MISTY: He was really funny, because people in the neighborhood respected him. A lot of these old school guys that would hang out on the streets and at the liquor stores, they'd talk to him, they knew who he was, he said. They would bring him like weed, like anything he wanted. He once told me, "If I was a drunk I'd have the best booze being brought to me from these young cats out here."

Because I always thought it was kind of dangerous for him to have that car parked downstairs, he was not a very healthy man. There was a lot of that Crips and Bloods shooting and drive-by thing going on in South Central back in the day. And he lived in the centre of Hell, I thought.

IAN: He lived on Crenshaw Boulevard, right?

MISTY: He did, 154th. When I say the shady part of the hood, it was like the centre of the jungle. It's interesting why he chose it after leaving [Betty] because they did have a house together before they split up in Hollywood.

He didn't go to an apartment somewhere in Los Angeles, or West LA. He packed up his little bit of clothes and belongings when they split and basically returned to the hood and that's where he remained. He felt good going back to the streets, so to speak, like another part of cleansing of his life.

IAN: How was his apartment?

MISTY: Oh my god, it was a horrible area, a horrible filthy building. His apartment was just full of books and junk. It wasn't lavish at all. It was a bed; I don't know what you call them in the UK, but just a single, like a bachelor, one room, a small kitchenette and a very tiny bathroom.

IAN: We call it a studio, everything in one big room.

MISTY: One *small* room! [Laughter] It was tiny shit-hole! And he was fine! He lived there for fifteen years. To him this is home. He was a recluse.

The man in the mirror

IAN: What did he drive?

MISTY: He loved classic cars. He had three different colours of Lincoln: a red one, a white one and a black one with the big white-walled tires. One was a 57, one was a 48. That was his black one. He sold them when my mom and him split. But he did keep the black one.

Even when he would go out to the market he would drive his huge old black Lincoln. That was the only thing he actually had that was something that showed that he had been a successful writer at one point.

So if he went to the market he would actually put his wig on and a nice pair of slacks with a button-up shirt. Then drive

135

this huge, very flashy Lincoln. People look at those cars, even if it's not pimped with the white-walls. People just tend to look at those cars because they stand out on a road. He would drive through the hood like that.

He never registered it since the 80s, which was funny, and he never got stopped! Didn't even have tags on it! He used to roll though with his Lincoln. He would pimp himself out just to go to the store even as an older man.

IAN: Was his Lincoln a convertible?

MISTY: His car was not a convertible... his wig would have fallen off. [Laughter]

IAN: Is it true that your mother made the clothes Iceberg wore on album cover of Reflections?

MISTY: She made all of his clothes. He would buy leather jackets or things like that, but she used to make him leather pants, she made him polyester – I mean that was really in in the 70s - all of his checkered suits. She would actually buy the patterns that he liked and she was a wonderful seamstress. She used to make our clothes as well.

IAN: Did he wear any favorite colours?

MISTY: No. He liked flashy... I mean he wore pink for godsakes! Guys are wearing pink nowadays but that was like crazy to be wearing it back then, it was extremely pimped out!

I think I have a picture of my brother wearing that [pink suit] as a joke when he was sixteen. Probably Halloween or something, but it was a hilarious suit.

He had an electric pink suit that was crazy funky, you know like Parliament had. It looked like a space suit because it was almost like pink foil. It was funny because he actually still dressed very much like a pimp.

IAN: And the wig?

MISTY: He wore the most awful wig that I can't tell you how awful it was because he lost his hair and he had the clown balding in the middle and he would wear this horrible, horrible wig.

He cared about his looks. He defiantly still had the need for the glare and flair of the pimp when his books started taking off. He did fall back at least into that part of the lifestyle, the clothes and things.

He would put an outfit together: it would take him longer to get ready than my mom! He'd be putting the wig straight and he would pull his face back with rubber bands on his ears under the wig.

IAN: Was that only because he wanted to market the books or...

MISTY: No. He really enjoyed dressing like that! Yeah, he could give up the dope and the hookers and everything, obviously, that was something he moved on from, but that was defiantly part of his personality.

You have Reflections; you've heard his voice. He's an extremely smooth talker and the way he dressed kind of went with the talk that he did, it kind of brought it out, the way that he spoke.

IAN: He still liked the jewelry and watches?

MISTY: Yes he did.

IAN: He had some degree of vanity...

MISTY: He used to say, "I'm pretty! I'm a good-looking motherfucker!" he used to say that all the time.

He would put his wig on when I would come over like, "Hold ooonnn!" and it'd be kind of crooked. And I'd bring a girlfriend, this girl Tiffany, with me. He really thought he was good looking and I thought that was kind of funny.

IAN: So he'd talk to himself?

MISTY: He's like "I'm a *pretty* motherfucker! When I was *young*..." I've got a picture of him when he was twenty three and he actually... I don't know if you're familiar with the way they used to shoot these actresses back in the silver screen days? They'd be looking away from the camera for instance.

IAN: Yes, looking to the side?

MISTY: Yes, looking to the side, black and white. I've got an absolutely gorgeous photograph of him. He really was kind of pretty, like the eyes: he had very, very, very alluring, deep, huge eyes that were extremely telling. There's a lot of sadness in them, but they were huge, he just had these huge eyes and in the picture he really is gorgeous. Yeah, I can see it. He still saw that person in the mirror, that's what was funny about him, because he'd be like, crusty; not up to par; laying around. He'd be kind of crusty sometimes and he'd be like, "I'm one of those cats that they just get *better*, you understand me!"

It was very interesting that he really took care of himself. He liked to look good, he was very well kept. Some people say that they look like clowns, but you know they put a lot of work into those color-coordinated suits and hats and the right shoes and the shine. It's their whole thing, their forte, their style. I don't know where that came from but it's been around since, you know, years.

IAN: I have an interview in which he states that he owned a little dog called Bill Bailey. Do you know who it may have been named after?

MISTY: I don't know who that is. He had a weird dog, a collie, when I was little, named Tina. My mom's Great Dane killed it.

IAN: The collie was his before he met your mother?

MISTY: No. When they got the house after the second book he actually... They bought those cars and he bought her mink coats. He liked jewelry: he had some beautiful gold rings, a gold watch.

They bought a huge Great Dane, which was extremely expensive, she wanted one. They are like horses, they are huge animals and he bought himself a *small* dog [laughs] it was like a Chihuahua. I have some pictures of it somewhere, it was a scruffy dog.

IAN: Did your father like to watch television or listen to the radio?

MISTY: He didn't like television as much as he liked reading...

138

IAN: What would he read?

MISTY: I don't know, but I know that he used to read the dictionary.

Betty and Bob: Honey and Ice

IAN: When we talked earlier you said that he rarely laughed, he wasn't a big laugher. What made him smile, what made him happy?

MISTY: [Laughs] Miles Davis! He would put some music on and he liked to smoke his pot and jam out to his jazz. You know his album [*Reflections*] had a jazz tinge to it. He liked that.

I always thought that he was more calm and mellow if he was waiting for a Laker game. He loved watching sports like basketball: it was a big deal for him. He was a big Laker fan for years and years. Even when they weren't doing so well he was a big Laker fan. So those are the worldly things that made him happy.

I don't think that he was happy. If you asked that to me and I didn't come up with those two things, which really aren't much: basketball and records. I don't think that he was ever happy and, unfortunately, I don't think my mom was either. And I'm really depressed because she just passed, because I think they could have done wonders and made films and optioned those books. If they would have went back together after the stormy part...

IAN: What caused the storm?

MISTY: My mother told me she was very upset that he never took her out to any of his book readings, or his lectures or anything, because he lied that she was Creole to the media. He called her Catherine in *Pimp*.

He wanted to throw the media off because she was white. Her name was Betty Mae Beck, by the way. The reason he did that, I believe, is because he didn't want any backlash from the Black Panthers, or even the white media, for having this interracial relationship that was looked on as being horrible.

There was a lot of attention and that's why I think that they split. Once his books did take off he wasn't around. He definitely had a taste for white women. He would be running around with white women in public anyway, the mistresses, if you will. So why not have your wife go with you? She's white as well. So if it was a big deal that people saw a black writer/pimp with a white woman, why not let it be your wife? That didn't make sense and ultimately it did break their thing into pieces.

My dad was really never the same after she left. He really loved her and he didn't want her to leave, but he really wanted to enjoy that spotlight.

Trick Baby was turned into a movie in 1973, I think. It was horrible. He did not appreciate that film. Unfortunately, he felt that they didn't do his story justice and it was really not what he would want out of the book. But it gave him a little thrust into the limelight again.

Unfortunately, you know, a man is a man. I don't condone any kind of cheating and I have never been one in my relationships, but... he was a man who had a very sexed-up lifestyle at one point: a young boy with cash and these women that would basically do anything. And he had that in him. A lot of men still love their wife and they'll stray and, again, it's not right. But I just wish my mom could have maybe... She never stopped talking about my dad and she missed him; loved him.

They were very stubborn people and I wish she would have kind of got over his philandering, but it really has to happen to you to make that kind of decision in your life. But I think she would have been better off to turn a blind eye a little bit and maybe let him enjoy a bit of what was going on. He was being invited to a lot of things.

IAN: Where was the name Catherine from? Was it a nickname from somewhere?

MISTY: No. It was just for the media. My mom wanted to be more in the public eye during their courtship. She said she had a lot to do with the books and she was this young woman, there's these movie premieres, Hollywood parties, why wouldn't she want to get out.

She had four kids she was at home with ninety percent of the time, so she had a lot of interest for that life, the cameras and stuff. You would imagine most women would want to be out there too, not to mention, she would probably want to keep an eye on him. That was kind of the demise of their relationship.

IAN: I've got down in one interview that he goes to watch *Trick Baby* with Betty and they keep their coats on ready to leave in case it's rubbish, but they stay and watch the whole film.

MISTY: Did he say that it was rubbish?

IAN: No. He praises it in a couple of interviews!

MISTY: [Laughs] This is a public interview?

IAN: Yes! [Laughs]

MISTY: When he's bought three Lincolns and a fur coat for his wife and the money...
     My mom especially was unhappy with the film, but he didn't think that it depicted his book, which is a contradiction to the interviews.
     Back then it wouldn't have been a good idea for him to say something like that if you want more of your books made into movies.

IAN: His situation was that *Pimp* was next up for being made into a movie. But back to what we were saying: it must have been hard for Betty if he was hardly taking her out with him.

MISTY: Yes, I think that was one of his mistakes and I believe that bothered him [after they split] that he didn't take her. He wasn't giving her the respect that, not only did she need, but I think she deserved, after helping him create his persona.

IAN: Do you think that it was difficult for him to make the transition into square life?

MISTY: Yes, although he said it wasn't. I believe that he had one foot in, and one foot out, of that world. And the only reason why one foot was in the real world is because he was writing and he had children and my mother yelling at him and the emotional stress of their relationship.

I truly believe that without the marriage and the children that he was sliding - not *ever* into putting women on the street again – but he was lavishing up in those parties. He was partying in the 70s after those books were published, he was happy. But he definitely still had that pimp thing going though, and I think that my mom couldn't accept it.

So I really didn't think he ever truly squared up, if you will. I think he'd like people to think that. But I think that it's such a deep-rooted thing, you know, what he went through and what he was. It's not easy to take that out of you. It's almost being like weaned out of the pimp mentality in that situation.

IAN: Were there any other factors affecting their relationship?

MISTY: He was never a big drinker. My mom had an alcohol problem during their relationship that she did get over in the 90s. But it was a driving force in a lot of their arguments.

One person is smashed off vodka and pills, which is my mother, and dad, he was completely stoned and mellow. I mean it was really like oil and water. You're stoned and you're just trying to hang out and kick back and relax and jot down some notes or read and then you've got this woman crying and drunk.

He didn't want me drinking because he said that I would have an alcohol problem; that it's hereditary.

IAN: Can you tell me about when your parents met?

MISTY: She had just arrived from Texas from an abusive situation. My mom was younger than him by sixteen years or so. He met her in Leimart Park in LA. She was working at a hamburger stand and he just kept coming there.

He had come into LA because his mother was dying; and she had come to LA get away from her own demons. When she came to LA she went to see her dad in Sherman Oaks, and that turned out to be a horrible meeting: her father was drunk and he tried to sexually molest my mom.

It was a time here in American when it was definitely something that wasn't looked on as good: to see a black man with a white woman. And my mom was typical white; southern; born in Virginia; grew up in Texas. And it wasn't a good thing for the public eye but they definitely had a connection. They dated.

My mom was pregnant with my brother when she met my dad. She didn't know she was pregnant when they met. He found out she was pregnant because, obviously, her belly was growing. I have a white half-brother.

My mom met my dad's mother before she passed. They lived in her house briefly while she was ill in the hospital.

IAN: What was Betty like?

MISTY: She was a very cynical, very dark-comedy-funny lady. My mom was very talented on so many levels. I wish you could have spoken to her Ian.

She was an amazing cook: she cooked a meal with low sodium, things that were sweet but didn't have all the sugar because he loved pies and things. She really took care of him so he didn't need the insulin shots 'till after they split and then he had to go on insulin. He did have bad kidneys on dialysis.

IAN: How much did your mother, Betty, say she was involved with *Pimp* and the other books?

MISTY: Listening to several [of her] stories of during their courtship, she was actually the one who suggested that he started writing. So she inspired him to start writing down these stories. She was there when they were coming up with these ideas for the novels and she was his typist. Obviously, once it gets to the publishing house the editors get at it a bit, but the rough stuff of all the novels she actually typed up for him.

He was a strange guy who used to write on paper plates, on napkins, on anything. He did longhand on note pads but he would write on paper plates and things like that.

IAN: How easy was it for him to get published?

MISTY: The one thing that my mom said she did help with was that she was actually the one calling around to find him a publishing deal. He was very let down; it took a minute to get

143

someone to look at *Pimp*. Holloway House had something in the LA Times where they were looking for new authors. Bentley Morriss [of Holloway House] even had a [black playboy] magazine called *Players* with all black women. She thought that was the perfect place to contact because of the street stuff he was already dealing with.

He was trying other outlets, but the times when he did try he wasn't getting too much respect, you know, coming out with this book called *Pimp*. They didn't want to read that shit, you know. They were like, "Who's this character?" So he was a little put off for about a year.

[Betty and Bob] really were a team unit. That's why I think he would have written more and really got a hold of his fame and integrity with her. Because she was somewhat of a manager/wife/homemaker. She had a lot of hats that she wore.

It was probably a big loss for him to have her walk out after a lot of his cheating and his running around. He became a recluse and not so much of a player because of the demise [of his relationship.]

IAN: After your parents split, your father met Diane Millman in 1980. He married her 1982.

MISTY: Diane, his second wife: she was a fan. Bentley gave him some mail from her. She was sending him pictures and stuff in the 80s. She's younger than my mom; she's only 62 so in the 80s she was in her thirties. She came on to him and that's how they met.

IAN: Do you know Diane well?

MISTY: I'm fairly close to her, no-one else talks to her in my family. I know that he loved her and she was there for him for ten years and she used to drive him to dialysis. And she didn't think he had any money, so she wasn't using him for anything; she was actually a really good carer for him. That was apparent.

IAN: They remained good friends after they split?

MISTY: They never really split. He was a strange character. He married her but he never lived with her. He didn't want to live there. She had this beautiful home that her mother had left her and it's a nice area in Hollywood and he never moved in with her. But I know that they were extremely close and she did a lot for him.

IAN: Once he and Betty split he never released any more books. But he continued to write?

MISTY: He really was broken up that my mom left him and he claimed that he wouldn't be able to write another book without her. But *apparently* he did write this *Night Train* and there were some other lost notes that were starting stories...

He wrote... we have one of his manuscripts... Camille and my dad were extremely close. He gave her a novel called *Night Train on Sugar Hill*. It's rough: it definitely needs a little tune-up and that's what usually a publishing house will send an editor in for and clean stuff up. He definitely wrote that. I've read the first few pages of it.

IAN: What's *Night Train* about?

MISTY: It's definitely years, I mean hyper-speed, ahead of the other novels. I believe the character is loosely based non-fiction. I think it's him [Robert Beck] because it's a guy, a black man, in Los Angeles, who has a daughter. I think it's about Camille actually. That's why he gave it to her... I think about five months before he died.

We didn't know if there was a book and he actually mailed it to her. She was staying in Michigan. He was very sick, he was going through dialysis and I think that's why he gave it to her. I haven't read the whole book.

IAN: Will it be released?

MISTY: Camille tried to get a book deal through about four years ago. I don't know what ever happened with that.

Unfortunately because of our proceedings with the attorneys there are four of us, four heirs, and she needs all of us to sign off. We're all part of it now because of the legal stuff that goes on with my dad's work. So, that's a book that maybe one day will come out.

Robert Beck with friend Mike Tyson.

Courtesy of Misty Beck.

MEETING ICEBERG SLIM: HOW'S TRICKS?

By Richard Milner

7th June 2009

I interviewed Iceberg Slim in his home about forty years ago - an interview he later came to bitterly regret. And thereby hangs a tale.

Parts of our taped conversation appeared in *Black Players: the Secret World of Black Pimps* (1972), a study of the hustler's world which I co-authored with my first wife Christina. But when Ian Whitaker wrote me in 2009 seeking a more complete version than the excerpts that appeared in our book, I was unable to accommodate him. The original interview had been published in an ephemeral and forgotten magazine called *Rogue* that went out of business decades ago. Even an extensive Internet search failed to locate a single copy.

During the late 1960s, my wife Christina and I interviewed pimps and prostitutes in the San Francisco Bay area for a study of their world, which they call The Life. Christina had taken a part-time job as a dancer in a "pimps-and-hos" hangout. Over five years, we invited many of the bar's regulars to our nearby flat, where we conducted tape-recorded interviews.

At the time, we were young grad students in anthropology at the University of California at Berkeley. Our reportage of the "player's" world over five years was eventually praised by social scientists for "important contributions to understanding this urban subculture" (*American Anthropologist,* vol. 76, p. 122, 1974.)

Our study was widely reviewed in the popular press, and even was featured on *Sixty Minutes*, America's top national news programme. It also became the basis of Christina's doctoral thesis.

A wide audience of black and white readers - including many prison inmates who seemed to have confused it with a textbook on how to pimp - bought 280,000 copies.

Almost simultaneously, *Gentleman of Leisure* (1972), a remarkable photo essay by Bob Adelman and Susan Hall was also published. Both books documented the existence of a

149

secretive, "underground" social system that exists nationwide, employing identical slang and values in American cities coast to coast.

At the time, this was truly an unknown world at the nexus of race, sex, and money. It had its own rules, norms, social system, and incomprehensible lingo, at least so far as white America was concerned. It was also the cradle of "rap" and "hip-hop" music, which became ubiquitous a few decades later. Although we had been unaware of each others' work, our two independent field studies were in perfect agreement.

Black Players is now a sought-after collectible that fetches up to $400 (£250) on the Internet. Our unconventional anthropology, however, resulted in my getting kicked out of the University of California. At first, the Anthro Department decided to pull the plug on both of us, but in a compromise deal, Christina was allowed to complete her degree while I was sacked.

I was told by my chairman, who feared losing the department's government grants and fellowships, that I had been spotted driving around the city at night in Cadillacs, snorting drugs with black pimps. When he pointedly inquired whether that was my idea of fieldwork, I replied that it was.

He believed that our edgy project threatened the Department's standing with the government, since we were receiving funds from the National Institutes of Health. He certainly would have preferred that we disappear to some village in Africa or New Guinea for a few years, as our fellow graduate students had done. But we thought that exploring and documenting a home-grown subculture in American "ghettos" was more urgent and relevant for understanding our own society.

Anyhow, the karmic wheel has turned again, and the University of California Press has just published my latest work, *Darwin's Universe: Evolution from A to Z.* (Ironically, in some parts of the country today, my book on Charles Darwin and evolution is considered as undesirable as the much earlier treatise on pimps and hos.)

At the time, we had, of course, read Iceberg Slim's book *Pimp: the Story of My Life* (1969), which was well known to the players and their women. No hustler's "crib" was without a copy of *Pimp* or a Billy Holiday recording of *My Man. ("He isn't true. He beats me too. What can I do?")* Slim's autobiography, not surprisingly, was never acknowledged by the *New York Times* as a bestseller; it was completely off the national media's radar.

So here we were, two middle-class whites (well, in my case, almost white: Jewish) exploring this topsy-turvy subculture, where "stables" of women were the breadwinners while their "gentlemen of leisure" were obsessed with flashy clothes, elaborate hairdos, and ostentatious "rides." Their subculture and language was like a funhouse mirror image of middle-class marriage and morality. Sex with the boss was doled out only as a reward to good earners.

Even if I had sought to interview the fabled Iceberg Slim, whoremonger and jailbird, I had no idea where he lived or how to get in touch with him. I was impressed by his glossary of black street language, even as I was compiling my own. His publisher, Holloway House, which specialized in little-known black authors' novels about street life, guarded his whereabouts as if he were the Dalai Lama.

Then, in 1969, not long after *Pimp* became an "underground" sensation, the editor of a sleazy newsstand "girlie" rag, appropriately entitled *Rogue*, called me from New York with an assignment. Had I ever heard of Iceberg Slim? Of course I had. I told the editor that the street hustlers spoke of him as the king of pimps. The coldest. The slickest. The baddest. Would I be willing to fly south to Los Angeles for a few days to interview "Iceberg" at his home? Yes, in a heartbeat!

The magazine editor, Peter Wolff, had been a school chum of mine at Queens College of the City of New York. Although blessed with brilliant literary talents, he had abandoned "serious" writing when he made a breakthrough discovery: if you had a camera, you could get beautiful women to take off their clothes! Photos of semi-nudes - quite innocent by today's standards - filled the cheesy "men's mags" he churned out, along with erotic fiction and spicy interviews.

Wolff had already arranged for my audience with the then-reclusive Iceberg through his publisher. A few weeks later, I found myself comfortably chatting with a very bright, amiable, and gentle man who was introduced to me as Robert Beck - a very different character from the heartless sociopath of his autobiography.

Milt Van Sickle, Slim's decent, caring editor, was protective, even reverential toward his star writer. He made it clear that he would not permit a hatchet job by any judgmental journalist, and carefully checked me out until he was satisfied that I would be simpatico.

Van Sickle drove me to Beck's home in a shabby Los Angeles neighborhood, where the writer was bedridden with advanced diabetes. I found him open, gracious, intelligent, serious, and wryly humorous. Clearly, however, in his own quiet way he considered himself a star, and wished that he didn't have to meet anyone in his present condition: ailing, aging, balding, and living in reduced circumstances.

A few years later, in the mid-1970s, I saw him on television on a national chat show, attempting to assume a refurbished public persona. Beck affected a ridiculously huge, frizzy Afro wig and dramatic eyeliner. As his daughter remarked to Ian Whitaker, perhaps when he looked in the mirror "all pimped out," he saw the dapper young player looking back at him. This late-in-life attempt to revive his street image seemed to me a bit pathetic - like an over-the-hill actress fussing over hair and makeup, as if that could somehow restore her faded looks.

In our interview, as in much of his writing, Beck presented himself as the improbable winner in a morality play - the ruthlessly cold bad guy who causes a lot of damage, is harshly punished for it, and then, triumphantly, achieves redemption through self-knowledge and the discovery that he has a warm heart after all.

Slim had become a doting father to his two young daughters, whom he indicated he would defend to the death from the kind of abuse that he had routinely dished out to women. He stressed that he never sought to glorify the pimp's ethos, but to portray it accurately to warn young black men against entering The Life. And yet, when he saw young players and hustlers on the street, he told me, he still could not resist wanting to correct their "mistakes" and teach them how to improve their Game.

He incongruously interspersed flashes of literary language with street idioms. For instance, when I asked whether he had any regrets, he replied that he wished he hadn't spent so much time "in durance vile" - a seventeenth-century term, meaning long incarceration, that was new to me.

Beck later came to deeply regret our interview when I appropriated bits of it for *Black Players* without seeking his permission. When our book appeared, he wrote a powerful essay about his anger and hurt feelings in *The Naked Soul of Iceberg Slim* (1971.)

As Beck spun the story in that book, his mentor, an older grifter and fellow prison-inmate called Sweetsend Pappy Luke came storming into his home one rainy day, brandishing a copy of *Time* magazine. Pappy was outraged when he saw the article, which was about our forthcoming book. Iceberg Slim was described in the magazine as one of our "informants" among many. (*Time,* Jan 11, 1971, p. 54-55.)

The article, as Slim summarized it in his essay about Pappy Luke, described the "anthropological fieldwork" Christina had undertaken while she worked as a dancer in a San Francisco bar. Slim recalled how Pappy Luke had raged at him: "How could you sucker off for that conniving white broad and let her dupe you into the fairytale bullshit in that magazine?"

Slim went on to complain in the *Naked Soul* essay that Christina was "a white dancer... in a San Francisco watering hole for mostly black pimps and whores. She... burgled gems of the pimp game from forty pimp skulls toward a Ph.D. and a professorship in anthropology... The [*Time* magazine] piece claimed that the dancer had interviewed me extensively. I had neither heard of her nor seen her in my life."

Slim went on to recall that Pappy demanded to know what he intended to do about it. His reply: "What can I do? Everybody I could beef to would be white. Do you believe the magazine publisher or the courts would care a good goddamn that she sliced off a piece of my black ass?"

Besides, Slim asked Pappy, why had this supposed rip-off so provoked the old con man's fury? So some white woman wrote about The Game after talking to some pimps, and lied that she had spoken with him as well. Slim rationalized that he had ripped off many women for hundreds of thousands of dollars, so what real harm had been done to him?

Pappy responded as if Slim was the idiot dunce of his class. He ranted about how Benny Goodman "masqueraded" as the King of Swing while he stole the soul of black music, how Sophie Tucker got rich doing Ma Rainey's and Bessie Smith's acts, and how black "music, folklore, and culture" had been systematically looted for decades by white writers, professors, and musicians.

153

When I read Slim's account in *Naked Soul* of this emotionally charged conversation, I could certainly see Pappy's point. Yet we had never imagined that we were some kind of culture thieves. We saw ourselves as translators or reporters who were giving black pimps a voice they had never had before.

Although we did a reportorial job that has stood the test of time, in retrospect it may seem presumptuous that we had appointed ourselves as the black pimp's voice. They already had a clear, authentic (and talented) voice, and his name was Robert Beck, otherwise known as Iceberg Slim. But I also knew that our book would reach white readers, social scientists, academics, and mass media that were closed to him. To the so-called "mainstream media," Iceberg Slim was, in Ralph Ellison's phrase, "the invisible man."

Beck became so fired up after "Pappy's" diatribe that he started legal proceedings against us, which horrified our staid publisher, Little, Brown & Co., of Boston. His attorney put me on notice that he intended to sue, claiming that our book was a fraudulent pack of lies, and that he was going to seek money damages.

In defense, I immediately sent him the published *Rogue* interview, with my apology for having neglected to do so earlier. Also, I included a copy of his signed release granting unrestricted permission to reprint the interview.

Of course, I never heard back from Iceberg or his lawyers. I understood his profound irritation in discovering that he had been tricked "by a nickel slick white broad," as he put it. Of course, he could not deny that we had quoted him accurately, and had respectfully presented him as a world-class authority on The Game.

But there's no denying that we conned him into becoming one of our informants in *Black Players* under the guise of promoting his own books. I confess that I derived a guilty pleasure in having tricked the king of the tricksters.

Cut to today, forty years later. Suddenly, there is renewed interest in this old interview, which no one had been able to locate. I searched my files, the Internet, and my storage cubicles in vain.

As a last resort, I called Peter Wolff's widow, Patty Galle, a high school teacher with whom I have remained friendly over the years. She held out little hope, as most of

154

Peter's irreplaceable collection of magazines and photos were long gone. Dozens of boxes had been tossed out over the years. I nagged her with phone calls but heard nothing for weeks.

Then, wonder of wonders: while doing laundry in her basement, Patty spotted a copy of the precious *Rogue* of June, 1969, peeking out of an old carton near her washing machine. She called me immediately, and so, thanks to Patty, my conversation with Himself has been miraculously resurrected.

ODIE HAWKINS ON ICEBERG SLIM

By Ian Whitaker

Los Angeles

18th June 2009

In order to put your recollections into context could you say how you knew Bob and during what years?

I could put my answers to questions about Iceberg into two phases: A) What I listened to as a kid in Chicago, 1950s. B) Conversations (years later) in Los Angeles, 1960s.

1950s

Any memories whatsoever of Bob back in Chicago would be fantastic for the reader, as I know of no "eyeball witness" to him doing his thing in the streets.

As a youngster (12-14) I was one of a number of Iceberg Slim's admirers. We lived in a "red light" area in Chicago and Iceberg was a role model. He wore beautiful clothes, drove a lovely car and had women fueling his lifestyle. Why wouldn't he be a role model?

The Chicago of my youth; featuring Iceberg Slim, Big Al, Mr. Tootsie Roll, Cash Black, and a host of others, was a "wide open" town. Certain areas, designated red light districts were in effect. Picture Amsterdam without government supervision. Iceberg was simply one of many at that time. Some would say that he wasn't even a major league player.

He did his thing; a pimp is always busy, but it seems that he didn't really attain super pimp status until *Pimp* was published.

On a purely personal note, I was being groomed by Big Al, a peer of Slim's, for my life in the Game. But I flunked out because I didn't have the specific character elements to become a member of the elite. Big Al, long since "gone home," explained what mind-fuckin' and subliminal conditioning could do, but he also included the necessary components of "Strippin' 'n whippin." And that's where I flunked out. I just couldn't bring myself to "strip 'n whip." Maybe it had something to do with tender thoughts about my mother and sister.

Do you remember what car Iceberg Slim had back in Chicago?

The car was probably a Coup de Ville Caddie, or as they were called colloquially, "a hog." But how many teenagers pay attention to car makes when the girls are flashing?

How would he dress?

Extremely well. One could almost say – conservatively. But expensively.

What was he called on the streets back then?

So far as I know he was always called "Iceberg Slim." Or simply "Slim" by those who knew him well enough to step to that.

Richard Milner, who interviewed Bob in 1969, told me that Bob stated Iceberg Slim was not his name in the streets. Misty Beck said in her interview with me that Iceberg Slim was a name created to illustrate Bob's persona in the book *Pimp*.
    You refer to Bob back in Chicago as Iceberg Slim. So any clarification, uncertainty or certainty from you about the name Bob used in the streets of Chicago would be valuable.

It was always "Iceberg Slim" for me. I didn't know his real name for years.
    I can really appreciate the information that your research has uncovered. The [existence of a] family comes as a complete surprise. I was never privileged to be exposed to that side of his life.

But then, I think I've made it quite clear that I was not a confidante, someone who hung out with Iceberg. He was an icon up there, and I was a small boy circling about. If I had known that he was destined to become a Figure, I would've paid closer attention to the details of his life.

Can you tell me about Baby Bell?

Baby Bell was yet another well-known pimp, like Flooky I and Flooky II, notorious drug dealers who also pimped. I only knew them by reputation.

1960s

How did you come into contact with Bob in Los Angeles?

I moved from Chicago to California in 1966 and became involved in a community theatre group, the Performing Arts Society of Los Angeles. Iceberg, Robert Beck, came to our theatre to pitch a play to the director. It didn't work out; but we connected. We were from Chicago and I knew him by reputation and from a distance. We had drinks a few times and talked.

What play was he pitching?

I have no idea what the name of the play was, that Iceberg pitched. The director's name was Vantile Whitfield. He moved on from our community theatre to become the head of an Expansion Arts Program in Washington, DC.

[Vantile Whitfield was a founding director of the Expansion Arts program at the National Endowment of the Arts in 1971. He was considered a dean of black theatre. He died 9th January 2005. *Washington Post*, 23rd January, 2005. Page C11.]

Do you remember him talking about The Life?

When he came to pitch his play at PASLA, he mesmerized us with his unique theories of supply and demand, economics,

America's elaborately constructed levels of Puritanism, etc., etc.

I have to say that his book, *Pimp*, and the others, never came close to capturing his true voice; the level of erudition, hipness, body language and nuances that his "personal lectures' conveyed. Robert Beck, the super-suave "Barack Obama" of his trade, explained what his kind of pimp did in socio-economic terms. Let me skip back to someone who spoke as a "commodities broker."

"Pussy is a completely renewable resource. What kind of society do we live in, that would place a 'sin value' on the opening of a woman's legs with the price of oil per barrel? Or, the hedging of a non-renewable resource of something like clean water." Pre-Green.

I'm paraphrasing a bit here, but I think you get my point. He did that, over and over. What I'm paraphrasing does not come close to the way he said it.

Did he indicate anything about his present relationships with the opposite sex?

I was not privileged to know anything about his relationships with the opposite sex. A girlfriend who lived in his LA neighborhood once told me that there was "this guy who lives down the street – looks at you in a way that makes you want to get down with him." I think that translates to "attraction" of some sort. Was he out of the loop at the time? I don't know.

From the information that I've received from pimp friends, pimping is almost addictive. We're not talking about "industrialized pimping"/the Nevada Mustang Ranch/brothel bit. But rather the psycho-thrill that a street corner (Mom 'n Pop Store) pimp gets from convincing a new bird to fly – in the direction he points.

Did Bob express any regret or other sentiments regarding his past?

Regrets regarding his past? I can say, with some confidence, that I heard enough what he said to be able to say that he would've been flabbergasted that someone would suggest that he had regret.

Later, after *Pimp*, he went onstage at different venues – I went to see one at Loop Junior College – to give "dramatic" presentations about the evils – Chicago – of the art of pimping. I don't think that a lot of the virginal undergrads were really hip to what he was getting at. Potential hoes, to be certain. Regrets? I don't think so.

The Loop Junior College Chicago presentation was well attended and I suppose one could say – dramatic. One tall, dark skinned man, with a receding hair line, a colorful scarf around his neck, talked about the trials and tribulations of an authentic pimp.

Sentiments about pimping, like the missionaries putting Mu Mus on the naked Pacific Islanders, is an acquired taste. Iceberg Slim played the game for what it was worth, but I don't think many of us "True Believers" went for the okey-doke.

Do you remember any stories he liked to tell or have any anecdotes?

I can recall Iceberg Slim talking, first when I was a street corner kid, and later as an adult. As a kid, on the fringe of conversations this man was having, I understood very little. As an adult, listening to someone talk about "pimpin' 'n hoing" as though it were the Stock Market – that was a revelation.

I was always struck by the poetic flow of his rhetoric. He was a brilliant man, a master psychologist, a gifted speaker. And had gone to college. He could've been a lawyer or a psychologist easily.

How was Bob dressed when you first met him in LA?

Robert Beck had creases wherever creases were supposed to be. He had his hat cocked ace deuce. He wore the proper pinkies and he radiated a mysterious kind of charisma.

Did diabetes apparently impact Bob's life when you met him?

I have no information about Iceberg and diabetes.

What appeared important to Bob in his life?

Money and all of the options it offers seemed to be the most important thing in Iceberg Slim's life.

Did you meet Bob again?

I got to know him a little better as a fellow member of the Open Door Program, a writing program started by guilt-ridden members of the Writer's Guild of America, West after they decided that there should be more writers of color in their Guild.

Do you know what year this would have been?

I believe that the Open Door Program was 1967-1970.

Was Open Door's purpose to facilitate writing screenplays or books?

The Open Door's purpose was mainly to facilitate screenplay writing, with books a distant second.

Could you elaborate on Bob's involvement in Open Doors? It was to improve his own skills?

Maybe he became involved in the Open Door Program (not doors: they were only willing to open *one* door at a time) to improve his writing skills, I can't say. But he was there.

I don't know if he wrote his *Pimp* while he was in the program; but we both wound up having books published by Holloway House. The LA New Times article has it exactly right when they say we, Blacks, built Holloway House. Donald Goines, Iceberg Slim, Joseph Nazel and Odie Hawkins.

I'm the last of the builders still on the scene. I have recently published books – *Mr. Bonobo Bliss* (Socio-Science-Fiction.) *Mr. Sweets*, the lifestyle of a pimp. And *Shackles-Across Time*, a look at the African involvement in the West African slave business.

Circa 1971.

Courtesy Holloway House Publishing Co., Los Angeles, CA.

QUESTIONS WITH BENTLEY MORRISS OF HOLLOWAY HOUSE

By Ian Whitaker

Los Angeles

May and June 2009

Could you describe Bob Beck's character? What kind of man was he?

He was bright, soft spoken, articulate, many times quite profound, immaculately dressed and an imposing 6ft 2. Loaded with ego and self-esteem.

Amongst the old articles I found, one said that after seeing an advert in the LA Times, Bob had dropped off his manuscript and returned later to collect his sunglasses, which he had left. Upon his return, Holloway signed him up. Is this a true story?

To the LA Times ad, Holloway House advertised welcoming new black authors to submit original manuscripts.

I'll tell you what occurred here almost 40 years ago. Holloway House had the reputation of befriending, welcoming and developing black writers. Literally hundreds of unsolicited manuscripts hit the office weekly and occasionally personal visits.

Holloway House was the place for black authors in those days. Beck certainly was aware of this. He visited the office and left sample chapters and a synopsis for our then editor Milt Van Sickle. Milt brought it into Ralph Weinstock's office (my Holloway House associate) with a high recommendation. Ralph made the decision to ask Beck back with the complete manuscript and it was Ralph who made the decision to publish the work.

Ralph had brilliant perception about such things but asked me to give it a run through. And it was I who confessed to Beck that some of his language was strange to a white honkey like me and suggested he create a glossary of "pimpdom" words. The glossary became one of the most quoted and talked about parts of the work. Bob was great to work with.

Was the success of Bob's first book *Pimp* a surprise to him?

The success of *Pimp* was not an overnight event. Notwithstanding, it was embraced in Los Angeles with awesome sales reception.

How did he react when you told him it was doing so well?

Bob was "cool." I'm sure he expected the work to be a national sales winner, but I think we were both pleasantly surprised on its mainstream acceptance.

You got Bob an appearance on the Joe Pyne radio and television shows...

A very, very popular talk show. It created a sensation. Our phones never stopped ringing.

Would so-called "normal" bookstores stock *Pimp* when it came out or were there issues with it being the type of book it was?

In the 70s and 80s in this country, black literature was not warmly embraced by so-called "normal" bookstores. But Holloway House helped in some small way to show Black America did read, had money, purchased books and was a profitable market to be addressed.

Holloway had over 400 black authors, including Robert Beck, that ultimately culminated in an African-American book section in leading bookstores throughout the North American continent.

What was the process of producing a book with Iceberg Slim? For example, did the ideas for other books come from Bob, or would he propose ideas?

Additional works beyond *Pimp* were ideas generated by Bob. He was not an aberration. Bob was a serious, dedicated writer.

166

We helped by a Christmas gift of an IBM electric typewriter and my personal gifts of the glossary suggestion and the title of his reflections, which became *The Naked Soul of Iceberg Slim*.

What were, apparently, Bob's motivations in his career as a writer?

Bob considered himself to be - and rightly so - a serious writer. He recorded some "rap," some original poetry, he made many personal appearances which Holloway House organized and was truly a creative exciting talent. He had a family to support and I think that was a major consideration in his life.

Did he change over the years since you first knew him and how?

Over the years he grew in understanding more about the "race" issue in this country.

Bob wanted to affiliate himself with the Black Panthers in Los Angeles but he was rejected by them as one who exploited black women. He was heartbroken.

Did you ever talk with him about how much of *Pimp* was true?

Never doubted one word as to the authenticity of his work

Did Bob mention if his original name in the streets was Iceberg Slim?

Bob did not discuss his "original name" in the streets.

Have you heard of the name Slim Lancaster?

Yes, I do recall Bob using the name Slim Lancaster, but can't recall where.

Can you tell me about the lecturing Bob did across the country at colleges and universities and how that came about? What was the purpose of these talks?

We have a very knowledgeable and aggressive publicity department and after some local inquiries and campus appearances we made Bob available for public appearances at every opportunity.

He loved the mass acceptance and the college kids ate him up with questions galore and always never-ending applause. Think. You've heard of pimps, you've read about them, but to meet one so cool, so majestic, so honest, so frankly intellectual - that's an experience to treasure.

And, of course, he played the role perfectly - gentle, soft-spoken, master of the language on and off the street. And Holloway House was more than pleased because they were there to sell books.

Did Bob usually attend his public appearances alone?

I do know Bob in his public appearances was not accompanied by any members of his family.

Did he talk about his personal life with you?

To my recollection in meetings with Bob, he never, but never, mentioned his daughters or his past and then present wife.

Is it true he spoke at Harvard University? I know his work was studied there as part of a class on "Rogue Literature" there, but I don't know if he went.

Was not aware of Harvard but I do know his book was ordered by the FBI, police departments, law enforcement agencies and college literature departments all over the country.

How would you describe his influence on literature?

As to the influence he generated in literature, I leave that to the academia pundits. I do know he influenced a whole cadre of rap artists, he brought into the fashion world the word "pimp" in describing design, he brought to light a sub-culture that heretofore existed on only police blotters.

How many books has Iceberg Slim sold?

Of all the titles?

Yes, the total sales of all of his books.

Of all the titles, several million.

Ian, I have some information that has never been revealed before. You can use it for the first time in print.

Bob always wanted his works in hard cover edition, which in the "hard world" is reviewed and critiqued in the columns and, for some stupid reason, held in higher regard.

Actually without our knowledge he offered a manuscript to a friend of mine, Charles Block, a literary book and film agent. It would be destined for hard cover. Bob received a $3,000.00 advance and then Charles for whatever reasons and apparently in his agreement could, and did, request the $3,000.00 returned.

Bob had already dissipated the money. As a proud guy he couldn't endure the embarrassment of not returning the advance and settled for paperback with us. He came to Holloway (me) and asked if we would return the money to Charles and consider publishing the book. Sight unread, but because we had such respect for his work, the check was issued to Charles and Holloway House published the work. It was *Death Wish*.

Wasn't Bob contracted to be published by Holloway?

Yes Bob was contractually committed to Holloway. He didn't fulfill his contract. But as you know he came to us when he needed help.

Why were there no more books released after *Airtight Willie & Me* during his lifetime?

Beck wrote seven books that we know he authored.

Have you heard of *Night Train on Sugar Hill*?

Yes I recall mention of the work *Night Train on Sugar Hill* by Misty and Betty during my one and only meeting with Betty.

As I recall, Betty with an oxygen mask dangling from her neck and puffing on a cigarette. She was a captivating, interesting, bitter lady. You see, Ian, she received none of the benefits of Bob's success. The work *Night Train* never surfaced to my knowledge.

Why was *Doom Fox* not published by Holloway House?

Our editors believed that *Doom Fox* was not written by Bob Beck and management didn't relish walking into a possible law suit.

Misty Beck has told me that a few years ago she was surprised to find out that *Pimp* had been optioned for a film, because the family were not informed of it by Holloway.

Holloway House had full and complete rights with no right of review by the author as to terms or monies in the sale of rights.

It was Holloway's mission to get as much money to the author that the traffic would bear. As a small publisher, aggressively positioned in a niche market I sold more works for film than many established New York publishing giants. My contacts with the Hollywood film family over the years worked to great advantage to Holloway House authors.

There were several options sold for *Pimp* over the years with appropriate payments made to the author, and after his death, to his heirs. And once again it was Holloway House that researched and announced to Diane and Melody that notwithstanding what the will declared, monies would be divided into four parts.

Melody and Misty Beck took you to court regarding royalties. What was the outcome?

There was a complaint brought by Diane (the second wife), Melody and Misty. Usual author - in this case the heirs - claim they were entitled to more money. Had no basis but they pleaded poverty to the court and the case was settled.

Holloway House felt it best to settle the case so sales of film options could go forward and to this I suggested - not the ladies or the court - that we could give up all rights and revert them to the heirs in 2010.

From what I understand, this is with the exception of the *Pimp* movie...

The rights to *Pimp* have been sold and the ladies received payment as well as Holloway House.

[The ladies] have no control, rights or comment regarding the *Pimp* forthcoming film. That particular sale took me years to consummate. And to be perfectly clear, all the publishing rights and subsidiary rights excluding *Pimp* and *Mama Black Widow* will revert to the heirs January 1st 2010.

Is the film of *Pimp* currently optioned going ahead?

Pimp has been optioned for film by a major independent with major money going to the four heirs. For the dollars they spent I would assume they will be moving forward to film.

Bob really wanted to see his book *Pimp* as a feature film but we sold *Trick Baby* first, which was released in the 70s by Universal Studios.

Did Bob tell you what he thought of the film of *Trick Baby* once he'd viewed it?

Bob never expressed a negative opinion regarding the film *Trick Baby*.

Footnote to the release was Universal's plan to fly him to major cities for book promotions and Bob was adverse to flying and that briefly dampened book exposure. Universal was very happy with the film's profits.

In several interviews in the 1970s Bob states a film of *Pimp* is going to be made and one article says he's writing a screenplay for it. Is that true? What prevented it from coming out so far?

Yes, Bob did take a stab at writing a screenplay of *Pimp* but it never went beyond the top desk drawer to my knowledge.

Imdb.com is showing that a film of *Mama Black Widow* is in production.

It took over five years of endless lunches, phone calls, e-mails and meetings to bring the project to a final sale.

Mama Black Widow was optioned and to the best of my information they should start the shoot in Chicago next month.

CREATING A PORTRAIT OF A PIMP

Jorge Hinojosa on his forthcoming
Iceberg Slim documentary film

By Ian Whitaker

Los Angeles

23rd July 2009

What is the name of your documentary on Iceberg Slim?

As of now, it is called, *Iceberg Slim: Portrait of a Pimp*.
Bentley Morriss made that suggestion and I thought it was
great.

Who is directing?

Me! I have never directed before but know a ton about Iceberg
and have watched a lot of documentaries. My confidence level
on doing the material justice is one hundred percent.
  I have also been encouraged by Ice-T, who after seeing a
seven-minute piece that I edited on Iceberg Slim, gave me his
blessing and encouragement. Ice is not shy in giving his
opinion, so his wholehearted endorsement boosted my
confidence.

How did the project idea come about?

I was first turned on to Iceberg Slim through Ice-T about
twenty-five years ago. As Ice started doing films one of the
ideas I came up with was to make a movie of *Pimp* with Ice
playing the lead.
  Unfortunately, the rights were owned by someone else.
Then with the threat of a writers strike happening in 2008 I
anticipated that there would be a lot of down-time and decided
to tackle this idea of a documentary on Iceberg Slim. I spoke
to Ice-T and he thought it was a good plan, so I dove in.

Is Ice-T narrating or involved otherwise?

Ice-T is one of the Executive Producers; he's also interviewed and will contribute music. His passion for Iceberg is also huge inspiration to ensure the documentary comes out brilliantly.

Have any documentaries influenced or inspired you?

Both *Fog of War* and *The Kid Stays in the Picture* gave a singular perspective, which is not the norm for documentaries and that I found intriguing. *The King of Kong* was hilarious and tragic. I think everyone in the US can relate to what was going on in that film, it was high school all over again. I thought all of these films were great.

What was Betty's reaction to the documentary being made?

She was really into it. I think she felt that it was an opportunity to make sure that Iceberg was celebrated and that she as his partner was given recognition for her contribution as well.

Can you tell the reader any interesting anecdotes from Betty that won't make it into the final film?

When I met Betty it was about ten months before her death, she was very sick and constantly in and out of the hospital. I was concerned about her ability to be interviewed, or to be understood, because her voice was incredibly raspy from years of smoking.

We interviewed her once but were not able to interview her a second time because she was just too sick. During our, one and only interview, she alternated between taking puffs of a cigarette and taking hits from her oxygen tank. Because pure oxygen is so incredibly combustible the crew was freaking out that she was going to blow us all up!

I had many conversations with Betty during those ten months. I spoke with her at least once a week. During one of those conversations she told me how the name Iceberg Slim came about. Contrary to the story in the book, she told me it was a name Iceberg invented. He chose it because he felt it was a fitting metaphor for himself because an Iceberg is cold and the majority of an Iceberg is hidden from view, so only a small percentage of the total mass is seen.

I was knocked out by that explanation but felt it was apropos. In doing the research for this documentary I have uncovered many things about him that he never reveled: things that would have boosted his credibility as a man of The Life.

Betty, like Iceberg, came from a dysfunctional family background. That and the love of books were the two biggest things they initially had in common, but unfortunately it was not enough to keep them together.

Did Betty or any folk from Chicago mention Baby Bell to you?

Yes, Betty talked about how both Robin and Misty were named after him. Diane also talked about how he was a great friend to Iceberg.

Did Betty or anyone say why the movie of Pimp *was not released after* Trick Baby *back in the 1970s?*

Back then a movie about a black pimp would have been too much for the public to deal with. Even now it's something a lot of studios would probably shy from.

What expectations should the moviegoer have going to see Portrait of a Pimp?

This documentary is a story of fascination – pimping - and a man's transformation – Iceberg - and how those two aspects were inexplicably intertwined with each other.

I think the moviegoer will be surprised at how important Iceberg Slim was to the black crime genre, black cinema, rap music as well as celebrities like Ice-T, Chris Rock, Dave Chappelle, Henry Rollins and others. His work touched many people, but because he was more infamous than famous relatively few people understand his influence on black entertainment and entertainers.

"*I feel so triumphant that at seventy-two that I've survived, 'cause I've got news for you, rhetorically: if a nigger, if a male nigger is able to survive in this society to be almost seventy-two, friend, he has accomplished one hell of a miracle. Believe me. Believe me.*"
Answer Me! Issue 1, by Jim Goad. October 1991.

Photo circa 1977. Courtesy PLAYERS Magazine, USA.